BUSING AND BACKLASH

BUSING

WHITE AGAINST WHITE IN A

UNIVERSITY OF CALIFORNIA PRESS

AND BACKLASH

CALIFORNIA SCHOOL DISTRICT

LILLIAN B. RUBIN

BERKELEY, LOS ANGELES, LONDON

UNIVERSITY OF CALIFORNIA PRESS
BERKELEY AND LOS ANGELES
CALIFORNIA
UNIVERSITY OF CALIFORNIA PRESS, LTD.
LONDON, ENGLAND

PRINTED IN THE UNITED STATES OF AMERICA
DESIGNED BY DAVE COMSTOCK

CONTENTS

PART FIVE: RACE, CLASS, AND DEMOCRACY

TABLES

ORGANIZATIONS

	Abbreviation
Association of Richmond Educators	ARE
Citizens Advisory Committee on De Facto Segregation	CACDFS
Citizens Committee for Neighborhood Schools	CCNS
Citizens for Excellence in Education	CEE
Congress of Racial Equality	CORE
Contra Costa Legal Services Foundation	CCLSF
Legal Action Committee for Equal Schools	LACES
Richmond Unified School District	RUSD
United School Parents	USP

PREFACE

I became interested in this study late in 1968 when local newspaper and television headlines called my attention to the fact that the community in which I live was mobilizing for political battle. As a sociologist, I had long been concerned that too many of our theories are spun in the heads of theorists who remain distant from the world they are theorizing about. As a political actor, I had been equally concerned about a democracy in which in most aspects of political life small groups of people, generally from the middle and upper-middle classes, make important public policy in the name of all the people but without their significant participation. It seemed that sociologist and politician had something important in common: both were distant from the objects of their endeavor — a distance that makes for facile generalizations and distorted perceptions. Simply stated: theories that are too far from the empirical data make bad sociology; political decision-making that is too far from the people is bad democracy.

The struggle in the Richmond Unified School District made it seem an ideal place in which to test these notions. I was already familiar with the area, having lived there for more than a decade and having shepherded a child through its schools. The community was sufficiently large and diverse to exhibit all the complex problems of any urban school system, yet small enough for me to observe the conflict process operate and to identify the strategic actors, so it presented a manageable research task.

It is always difficult to know how and why a book comes together in a particular way. At one level, it is the culmination of a lifetime of experiences. But in the day-to-day business of writing and revising, family, friends, and colleagues make their mark. Thus, this book is better, stronger, and, I hope, more honest for the critical readings of Ann Bardacke, James Benet, Bennett Berger, Fred Block, Arlene Daniels, Fred DuBow, Sandra DuBow, Carole Joffee, Dorothy Jones, Louise Kapp-Howe, William Kornhauser, Michael Leiserson, S. M. Miller, Bruce Miroff, Philip Selznick, Rodney Stark, Ann Swidler, Robert Wood, and Will Wright.

To Troy Duster I owe a special thanks for having faith in my work when some did not. To Irving Rosow, whose disagreements were loving and whose criticisms were constructive, my warmest gratitude. To Michael Rogin, teacher, colleague, and friend, who read the manuscript from first draft to last, I owe a most important intellectual and personal debt. His excitement about my work and my ideas sustained me through some difficult times. His insightful criticisms were always stimulating and thought-provoking. This book is substantially enriched by my association with him.

Grant Barnes, my editor, has the intelligence and sensitivity to make what is traditionally a difficult relationship into a pleasurable one. His capacity to criticize my brainchild without making me defensive helped make this a better book. For that, and for guiding the manuscript through the mysteries of publication, I am grateful to him.

Finally, there are two others — my daughter Marci, and my husband, Hank — whose love, support, and faith sustained me through the whole project. This book could not have been written without them. They listened patiently while I tried out my ideas; they encouraged me when I was right; they argued without restraint when I was wrong. Marci, student of political theory and the law, brought her fine, critical mind to bear whenever it was needed. Hank brought to every problem a lifetime of radical criticism of the American political scene, a sharp wit, and an extraordinary capacity to make sense and simplicity out of complexity. By now he must be at least as familiar with every facet of the book as I, since no word escaped his keen editorial criticism. For all that there is really no way to thank them adequately. Thus, this book is dedicated to them with my love.

PART ONE

THE PROBLEM AND
THE SETTING

CHAPTER 1 **INTRODUCTION**

Let them send their damn buses; no kid of mine'll ever ride 'em. Not if I have to get out there and stop those buses myself. No one has a right to tell me what I can do with my kids. We made 'em, we had 'em, we support 'em, and we're entitled to do what we want with 'em.

So spoke a leading opponent of busing in the Richmond Unified School District (RUSD). "Racist bastards!" was the typical angry retort of the proponents. And the stage was set for the battle that would stop the buses.

The RUSD lies on the eastern shore of the San Francisco Bay and encompasses 110 square miles and several communities. Like most urban school districts in America, it has for years been organized around the small neighborhood elementary school. Consequently — again like most of its counterparts across the land — its schools are segregated by both race and class, reflecting the composition of the neighborhoods in which they are situated.

After several years of pressure from black community organizations and their white allies, in December 1968, under court order to desegregate one elementary school in the black ghetto (Verde School) which had served as a test case, the RUSD board set in motion plans to integrate all its elementary schools. Given the size and the configuration of the district, given the location of the dominantly black schools inside the ghetto on the western edge of the district, the plans necessarily included some two-way busing; that is, some white children would be bused to black ghetto schools, and some blacks would be bused to schools in white neighborhoods. Four months later the proponents of that plan were soundly defeated by the electorate, and the newly elected school board, composed entirely of anti-busing conservatives, rescinded the plan in favor of a voluntary open enrollment scheme.

With those few sentences, the salient facts have been stated, but they tell nothing of the turmoil, the polarization and, indeed, the political convulsions that preceded that outcome. A school district that historically had been governed by moderates or by a moderate-liberal coalition — people drawn from the "respectable establishment" of local business, professional, and PTA leaders — was suddenly engulfed in a conservative wave; dominated now by men who were little known before, avowed conservatives,* most of whom insisted that they owed allegiance and representation to a single sector of the area's electorate — their dominantly working-class and lower-middle-class conservative constituency.

Even while acknowledging that America's racial fears

---

* I use the designation *conservative* because that is the word with which all the men and women who were leaders in this movement described themselves, and because it is the term commonly used in American political life to describe their political characteristics and beliefs.

and hostilities stood at the center of the controversy, the outcome was puzzling. Specifically, I sought the answers to such questions as: What were the weaknesses in the moderate-liberal coalition that facilitated such a complete ouster from power? Where were the critical junctures at which they either acted incorrectly or failed to act at all, thereby contributing to their failure to retain power and to integrate the elementary schools in the district? What were the ambivalences and strains, the structural and ideological sources of their failure? On the other side: What were the strengths that enabled the conservatives to mobilize what formerly had been a relatively apathetic constituency? What accounted for the politics of rage so evident in the struggle over the schools in the RUSD? What, in substance, gave the "silent" majority its voice?

These questions are more than academic. The RUSD is in many ways America in microcosm, and its agony reflects the pain in the land today. Busing school children to correct racial imbalance is perhaps the hottest issue in American politics, and public retribution against those who favor busing plans is swift and sure. Even the courts are not immune, as witness the defeat in November 1970 of Judge Alfred Gitelson of Los Angeles, a twelve-year Superior Court veteran who had ordered the integration of the Los Angeles schools * — a lesson that has not been lost on our representatives in Congress. There, on November 4, 1971, in an extraordinary session that lasted until 2:30 A.M., members of the United States House of Representatives voted overwhelmingly (235–125) to prohibit the use of any federal

---

* Even though Judge Gitelson's opinion did not contain one word about busing, he was defeated in a bitter election campaign in which his opponent, William P. Kennedy, hammered away at one theme only — his own opposition to busing school children for racial balance. The implicit promise of the Kennedy campaign was that by defeating Gitelson his ruling would automatically be overturned, and the voters eagerly bought the promise.

funds for busing, to forbid federal officials to pressure local school board to use their own money for busing, and to permit the delay of court-ordered busing until all legal appeals have been exhausted.* Many northern liberal Democrats, who until then had been articulate spokesmen for school integration, cast their votes for these anti-busing amendments; others left the floor to avoid being counted. Watching this performance, their southern and Republican colleagues shouted and applauded gleefully. During the debate, Representative Edith Green, an Oregon Democrat acknowledged to be the foremost House expert on education, spoke:

> We cannot go back a hundred years to make up for the errors of our ancestors. The evidence is very strong that busing is not the answer to our school problems.

In reply, Representative John Conyers, a black Democrat from Detroit, charged:

> . . . this is not only unbecoming conduct, but it is the height of hypocrisy and cowardice working hand-in-hand.

And Shirley Chisolm, black congresswoman from Brooklyn, said angrily:

> Let me bring it down front to you. Your only concern is that whites are affected. Come out from behind your masks and tell it like it really is. Where were you when black children were bused right past the white schools?

And, indeed, Americans had been silent all those years — a silence for which we are now paying the price as we struggle to redress that injustice.

---

* The Senate must approve these amendments before they become law. Most political observers suggest that cooler heads will prevail in that body where members, because they serve for six years instead of two as in the House, are less subject to immediate pressures from the electorate.

In Richmond, a community sensitized by its proximity to Berkeley, the first city in the nation to institute a two-way busing program at all elementary grades, residents were fearful and on guard. Thus, the first hint that the school board was considering integrating the elementary schools brought immediate hostility. Opponents argued — as they have across the nation — that they were not opposed to integration, but only to busing. But given the reality of housing segregation, to oppose busing is, for all practical purposes, to oppose integration. And, in fact, if one looks at the record, it is clear that it is not busing alone but busing for integration that is resisted so tenaciously. One leader of the anti-busing movement in Richmond said it clearly:

> I would do everything in my power to resist it. . . . *Under no circumstances will my kids ever ride a bus for even one minute for the purpose of integration.*

When I asked, "What would you allow them to ride a bus for?" he answered, "For overcrowding or any other such *reasonable* reasons for which children ride buses. *But not for integration.*"

Lest his attitude seem to be some personal aberration, the record shows that in an earlier dispute over whether to unify the school district, opponents of unification in Pinole (a city within the school district) feared that under a unified system Pinole "might lose all bus service even in elementary school areas."[1] Moreover, one of the men who spearheaded the anti-busing movement and who in that context argued vehemently that it is hazardous to the life and limb of children to ride a bus to school, six months earlier had demanded that the school board furnish bus transportation for junior high school students in his area because walking to school was too hazardous. Finally, throughout the district's history, several thousand white elementary school pupils — most of them from those areas where resistance to busing for integration was highest — have been bused to school daily without protest from their parents. Since several of those parents were leaders in the anti-busing movement, I asked them if they did not see some contradiction. Most were made uncomfortable by the question, and, although they all denied any inconsistency in their position, none was able to reply convincingly. One said, "Well, there's no school closer, so it's all right. It's not as if the children are being bused by a closer school to go out there." Another, "I oppose forced busing and *that's not forced busing because there's no choice now*. We don't have a school in this area." And a third, "Busing is acceptable now because it's close, and because they're going into an area where I know the community and where the goals are the same as ours. . . . Myself, I want my child to be in school with people like himself."

Reminiscing about these matters, a former long-time school board member said:

> It's funny how times change. When I came on the board, there was a very large (for that time) screaming, shouting meeting. The issue was that people were demanding buses because a little girl had been raped on the way to school. So they wanted the school board to supply buses as a matter of safety so that no child would have to walk farther than from his home to the nearest bus stop. It's only when you're talking about busing for integration that busing becomes an issue.

The political divisions in Richmond also reflect those in the state and the nation — intense polarization between liberal and conservative that often is rooted in class differences that give rise to disparate ideologies, world views, life styles, and values. Thus, once the controversy over integration brought the two groups into conflict, their different viewpoints on other school issues surfaced to reveal differences in attitudes about financing the schools and about the kinds of educational programs they should offer. Accordingly, as large numbers of formerly inactive working-class and lower-middle-class people were mobilized around the issue of integration, their concerns about sex education in the schools, "decency in literature," educational television, teaching the three Rs, and what was characterized as the profligate spending of the incumbent school board were brought to public attention.

It was not long before the cleavage grew so deep that many participants on both sides were pushed to what seemed to them to be extreme positions, often against their will. "Those in the middle were driven to one side or the other. I was one of those. It was awful." So spoke a former board member, a self-defined moderate, and one of the first to be defeated for reelection in 1967 on the busing issue. On the conservative side, one of the most prominent leaders said, "Ten years ago I considered myself a moderate-to-liberal Republican. Now I would have to label myself as a moderate-to-conservative Republican. As the liberals moved more to the left, I felt I had to be a counterweight."

Meanwhile, as the public response to their initiatives grew, conservative leaders began to flex their political muscles. For the first time they realized that the schools themselves were within their grasp. Not only did they have the numbers to stop integration, but also to wrest control entirely from the liberal-moderate coalition then in charge, thus permitting them to implement their own educational philosophy.

Complicating the political and racial antagonisms was the fact that the RUSD had been created in 1965 in response to state pressures for the unification of school districts. The schools from five separate cities and six unincorporated territories were brought together in a single administrative unit. But that administrative change brought with it little social or political cohesion. Instead, unification created an artificial political organization which was superimposed upon a heterogeneous area whose constituency perceived few, if any, common bonds; a political unit devised to meet the goals of economy and efficiency, but with little regard for the history and diversity of the people who would live under its jurisdiction; a school district that was headed for trouble from the moment of its birth.

THE RESEARCH PLAN

Sociological studies usually end with a methodological statement. I choose to begin with one because in order to evaluate what follows, the reader should know how I did the research, where my data came from, and how I gained access to a resistant population. At the outset, however, it should be understood that such a retrospective statement of the methods of the study always makes it sound neater and more controlled than it really was.

The data for this study were collected over two years, mainly by field observation and interviews, but also through examination of school district documents, election returns, newspapers, and periodicals.

On December 18, 1968, I attended my first meeting of the RUSD school board, a meeting that filled Richmond's Municipal Auditorium to capacity with about 3,500 angry people. At that meeting the school board voted 3-2 to adopt an integration plan that included two-way busing. The rage was so explosive, the din so fearful, as to defy description. Indeed, it may be best summed up in this chaste little sentence from the minutes of the meeting: "Other speakers did appear briefly, but because of the degree of noise it was not possible to obtain their names."

In fact, by that time neither side was interested in hearing what the other had to say. It was soon to become clear to me that it had been almost two years since a public discussion about the schools, at school board meetings or elsewhere, had resembled anything but a pre-game rally — each side speaking more to buoy up its troops than to persuade the other, each side exhorting its followers to ever greater feats of daring. Slogans and epithets were the language of discourse, all to the simultaneous accompaniment of loud shouts of approval and hoots of anger from the audience. A divided board added to this circus atmosphere by snarling at each other and at people making presentations from the floor that were not to their liking.

A month or so after beginning my observations, I contacted the superintendent of schools, a liberal reformer committed to integrating the schools, and requested cooperation. Like all the liberal participants in this study, he assumed (not incorrectly) that I was on his "side" and asked one of his chief aides to provide me with whatever information I might need. This working arrangement lasted only a few months, however, for when the new conservative school board took office July 1, 1969, they replaced the superintendent with a man who had been deputy superintendent for some years, a local man who had been with the district for more than thirty years and whose conservative loyalties were unquestioned. By that time, however, I had already been given copies of the minutes of school board meetings from 1965 to 1968 (the years during which the conflict was developing) and of relevant school district documents and publications; and I had developed informal relationships with several people in the administration.

From the outset it was clear that the new school board had little sympathy for any university-based research, and less yet for the discipline of sociology. In fact, the disputed integration proposals (among other things) were written off contemptuously by them as "sociological experiments dreamed up by those ultra-liberal sociologists at the universities." So great was their hostility to the University of California at Berkeley that when some faculty members and graduate students in the College of Environmental Design offered to develop plans for an educational-recreational complex on vacant land adjoining one RUSD school (plans that would cost the district nothing and for which they would assume neither responsibility nor obligation), the board debated for forty-five minutes before reluctantly agreeing by a 3-2 vote to accept the offer. Disturbed, one of the dissenters said in closing, "All right, but I don't want to invite the University of California to take on the use of this property as a project. I don't want to have anything to do with them, and I don't want to encourage or support them in any way."

Given these attitudes, I was certain that I would be refused if I asked for cooperation from the new superintendent. Since I feared that once I was openly refused the sanction of the superintendent's office, my contacts in the administration would hesitate to talk with me, I decided that it was wiser not to meet him and to go about my work as quietly as possible. Thus, I had no formal administrative cooperation during most of the research, although I did continue to call on some informal contacts within the administration from time to time. But those contacts soon became quite guarded and careful about the information they would pass on, and their usefulness was limited.

My observations at board meetings acquainted me with the community groups and organizations who were participating in the struggle, and I began to attend the public meetings of several of them. Since during that time all meetings dealing with schools were very well attended, I was not especially noticeable. In fact, later, during the interviewing phase of the research, those respondents who had noticed me commented that they had thought I was a teacher.

After about a year, I made the first move that would

identify me as a researcher. I approached the presidents of the major organizations on both sides of the conflict, told them that I was writing a history of the school district since its unification in 1965, and requested permission to attend their executive board meetings. The president of Citizens for Excellence in Education (CEE), the upper-middle-class, liberal pro-integration organization, immediately invited me to their next board meeting and kept me informed of meetings thereafter. The president of United School Parents (USP), the working-class and lower-middle-class, conservative, anti-integration organization, replied that he would have to seek the approval of his executive board and would let me know. Several telephone calls and many months later, he still had no answer for me. My request was never refused directly, nor was it ever granted—just evaded.

Eighteen months after I first went into the field, I embarked upon the interviews. The desire to understand both the structural and ideological sources of the conflict dictated that I reach out to the most informed segment of each of the two publics, to those who could articulate their positions with the most clarity and consistency—the leaders.

But there were problems. The working-class and lower-middle-class conservative leaders tended to be suspicious, to look warily upon strangers, and to resist talking with anyone they thought might not agree with them. They felt that they had been maligned by both the press and the academic world and were distrustful of both. Liberals generally write off these fears of academia as paranoiac. I would argue, instead, that it is not paranoia but a realistic assessment that members of the academic community generally are integration-prone liberals who find it difficult to give the conservative position a fair hearing. Indeed, that is true of me as well.

I have been a lifetime critic of racism in America and an active advocate of an integrated society. Thus, I came to this study favoring the plan to bus children to achieve racial balance in the schools. I supported the proponents of that plan, voted for them, and was saddened by their defeat. For an upper-middle-class professional like me to view the world from the perspective of what the media call Middle America is, to say the least, difficult. The requisite empathy is elusive because too many experiences, beliefs, and values divide us. Yet as I talked with these working-class and lower-middle-class people, I began to understand that their behavior was not so irrational as distance made it seem. Their hopes, their dreams, and their fears began to be comprehensible.

Given the conservatives' suspicions, I knew that I would need two different approaches to the two different groups, one that played down my university connection for the conservatives and one that played it up for the liberals. Experienced field researchers warned me that it would not work, that so long as there were any people in the area who knew the truth about my mission and my university identity, it would be impossible to keep them secret. The whole project was at stake. If I made a straightforward declaration to the conservatives, I was certain that they would not talk to me. On the other hand, I already had evidence that polarization was so complete that communication between the two warring camps was nonexistent. For I had lived in the district about ten years and a few of the key liberals — neighbors and friends — knew both my identity and my mission, and although it was then eighteen months after I had begun the project, no word about me had leaked to the conservative side. I gambled on using the two different approaches and was soon to discover that I need not have worried, since I was apparently the only person to cross the chasm separating the two groups in several years. While within each camp the grapevine worked very efficiently and my visits and activities were subjected to lively discussion and scrutiny, there was no transmission of information across the lines.

I told the conservatives that I was writing a book about the history of the school district and that I wanted to talk to them because they were making that history. In general, they asked for no explanations of my purposes beyond that statement. But they wanted reassurance that I was on their side in the fight over busing, that I did not think sex education belonged in the schools, that I had not favored unification of the district, that I was not, in short, "one of those liberals." Naturally, I refused to answer those questions and only assured them that I would try to give their side a fair hearing.

It often took fifteen or twenty minutes on the telephone before I could persuade a conservative leader to make an appointment; and a few refused to see me at all. Despite their qualms, once they agreed to an interview, they were eager to talk and to justify themselves, feeling a sense of importance at being asked their opinions and at being listened to so attentively.

In direct contrast to the conservatives who feared the university, many of the liberals wanted assurance that my research was university connected before they would cooperate. If I were just another journalist, they said, they could not be certain of my objectivity. One need not look for differences in the psychological predispositions of the two groups to understand their responses; the reasons are quite clear. All the liberals were university educated and university oriented; some were professors at Berkeley; and most were convinced that there is an almost mystical objectivity in social research emanating from the university. Such beliefs were easy for them to hold since, unlike the working-class and lower-middle-class conservatives, most of the research findings dealing with social issues support their values, beliefs, ideologies, and life styles.

In all, I interviewed fifty people: the eleven men and women who had served as board members since the unified district was organized; the twenty leaders (either elected officers or committee chairmen) of the two major organizations on either side of the conflict; four leaders of the only racially integrated organization in the district; and fifteen more people who were a mix of teachers, administrators (including the ousted superintendent of schools), and others who had some special knowledge about the events by virtue of the centrality of their roles.

Except for the sociodemographic data that I gathered on each respondent, I approached the interviews with a very loosely focused guide — that is, with some guidelines for directing the conversation into the most productive channels for my research questions. While in the interest of comparability, a few standard questions were asked of everyone, by and large, I had a different set of guidelines for each group of respondents. Moreover, since many of the respondents were privy to special information because of their special roles in the struggle, I often found it necessary to tailor the guidelines to the individual I would be interviewing.

The interviews lasted no fewer than two hours and sometimes as many as six. I met most respondents in their homes at times when they were relaxed and felt free to talk. Frequently the respondent's spouse sat in on the interview, quietly at first, but joining in more as rapport was established and the atmosphere became relaxed. Since I arrived with no printed questionnaire, no paraphernalia but a note pad, the mood was easy, and the interview was much like a leisurely conversation.

This, then, is a book about what I learned from watching the people in the Richmond Unified School District, from talking with them, and from reading about them for two and a half years from December 1968 to June 1971. It is a book about how human actors caught in a series of social-political dilemmas moved to resolve them. I do not expect the people on either side always to like what I have written about them, but I hope at least they will conclude that I have been fair.

PART TWO

THE BACKGROUND TO
CONTROVERSY

2 A SCHOOL DISTRICT IS BORN

Through a variety of incentives, mostly financial, the State of California for some years has been encouraging small school districts to unite with their neighbors. The reasons for the thrust toward unification are various and complex, and include the fact that many small rural districts often cannot offer the full range of graded classes and comprehensive high schools, both highly valued by most modern educators. This, coupled with the belief that larger school districts would be more likely to respect the professional status of teachers and administrators and more able to translate that respect into higher salary scales, won the support of professional educators throughout the state.

But whereas the state talks about educational considerations, its interest in economy and efficiency is more immediate and compelling, for the smaller districts are frequently impoverished, and the state is obliged to supplement their funds. By combining the resources of several small districts, the resulting single, larger unit could be expected to operate more economically and efficiently, and it would be more likely to have a tax base which would meet the state's minimum standards, thus relieving the state of its financial obligations to the separate districts. The latter is almost always the outcome when one of the partners to unification is an urban area with an industrial tax base (like Richmond) — a situation in which the state exerts maximum pressure.

The progress toward unification in the state was slower than policy-makers had hoped, both because the local citizenry was jealous of local prerogatives and because political subdivisions — including school districts — do not readily participate in their own demise. By 1963, therefore, the state recognized the need to add force to its policy of encouraging unification if that program were to succeed. So legislation was enacted that provided that any school area that had separate elementary and secondary school districts whose boundaries were coterminous had to hold a unification election every two years until unification was accomplished.

The elementary schools in the geographic area of this study had been organized in four separate districts (Pinole-Hercules, Richmond, San Pablo, Sheldon*), while secondary education was provided for the entire area by the Richmond Union High School District. Thus the area became a target of the state's unification drive. To sweeten the pie, the state offered some minimal financial incentives — a decreasing supplemental support program for the first five years that called for a 5 percent increase for the first fiscal year of the unified district's existence, 4 percent for the

---

* The Sheldon district had four schools, all in El Sobrante.

second fiscal year, 3 percent for the third, 2 percent for the fourth, and 1 percent for the fifth fiscal year after its foundation.[1]

THE UNIFICATION ELECTION

Under the mandate of the new law, the Contra Costa County Committee on School District Organization drew up a unification plan and ordered the four elementary school districts in the area to hold an election on that plan. The question was put before the voters November 3, 1964. By a 54 percent margin the proponents of unification won the day, and the Richmond Unified School District (RUSD) was born.

Examination of Table 1 shows that only the Pinole-Hercules voters defeated the unification proposal, with about 69 percent voting no. In Richmond and San Pablo, the proposal carried by approximately 57 percent and in Sheldon, by 66 percent.*

The campaign was desultory and uninspired. The measure was at the bottom of a long ballot on which voters

Table 1. Vote on Richmond School District
Unification Election, November 3, 1964

School District	Percent		Total
	Yes	No	
Pinole-Hercules	31%	69%	8,144
Richmond	57	43	35,835
San Pablo	57	43	9,864
Sheldon	66	34	3,148
TOTAL	54%	46%	56,991[a]

SOURCE: Contra Costa County Election Department.

[a] The 56,991 votes cast represented approximately 70 percent of the registered voters in the district.

* The schools in Sheldon, a white working-class and lower-middle-class suburban district, and in San Pablo, a dominantly white working-class city with a very limited tax base, were in deep financial trouble for which unification seemed to promise relief.

were asked to express their preference in a heated presidential battle (Johnson *vs*. Goldwater), and which contained fourteen state propositions, including the much controverted anti-fair housing measure, Proposition 14. Neither opponents nor proponents of unification presented compelling arguments. The former argued from a "save-local-control/stop-big-government" perspective; the latter retorted, "We don't really have a choice; this year or next, what's the difference?"

Substantively, proponents made two major arguments. First, they claimed that unification would ensure a better and more uniform education for all children in the district.[2] One informant who was a member of the Richmond Union High School board at the time, said:

> I supported it because the kids in those [suburban] districts were getting a lousy education. It was demonstrably different from what the kids in the Richmond schools were getting; they were going into our high schools, and we could see it.

But for some proponents of unification — largely people from the urban Richmond district — underlying that argument was the vaguely paternalistic notion that it would benefit the society to end the parochialism, insulation, and isolation of the suburban elementary schools. For in their view, these were not just *any* suburban school districts; they were largely working-class and lower-middle-class areas, peopled by (in the argot of the district) the "Okies" and the "Arkies," or their descendants, who had come to work in the Kaiser shipyards in Richmond during the early years of World War II. One prominent supporter of unification explained:

> The good guys voted for unification in the belief that the suburban districts would benefit from being drawn into an

urban and sophisticated educational system, that this would help end their parochialism and ultimately redound to the benefit of the whole society.

Second, they argued that unification would provide important financial advantages to the communities. It would "achieve a better tax base, a greater equalization of tax burden, and improved financial support for the schools at the local level, and improvement in the level of state support without increasing state taxes."[3] All the arguments for financial advantage emphasized the economies of scale — that is, the bigger district would be able to operate more efficiently, hence more economically. The local daily newspaper, the *Richmond Independent*, editorializing in support of unification, summarized that position aptly.

> . . . unified funds can be put to better use for the improvement of the overall educational program. There can be no doubt that the development of one budget instead of five will be advantageous; the management of supplies and equipment under unification will be more efficient; the amounts of bookkeeping and accounting in one large district will be less than needed in five districts now.

But there is still a third reason for supporting unification to which some in the district point, one that was never articulated in the debate, but which may be most relevant to the thrust of this study. The original Richmond school district (composed of Richmond, El Cerrito, and Kensington) had a black school population of roughly 40 percent. The 1960 census shows San Pablo with a population of 19,644, of whom 1 percent (196) were black, while it shows Pinole having a single black in a population of 5,860. Unification, therefore, had the potential to decrease the proportion of black students in the Richmond schools from about 40 percent to 25 percent. Pointing to that fact, one administrator with long tenure in the Richmond district explained:

> With the pressure for integration rising, many whites in that district [Richmond] were eager to dilute the black population by incorporating the almost completely white suburban areas.

Almost every white anti-integrationist respondent in this study said he had opposed unification and, without being asked or prompted, spontaneously offered the same belief as one reason for their opposition — a belief that was shared by at least one white integrationist leader, who said:

> It's one thing to integrate schools with a 25 percent black population; another, when the blacks are 40 percent and rising. People didn't talk openly about that during the [unification] campaign, but it was there — whispered about and on people's minds.

ORGANIZATION OF THE NEW SCHOOL DISTRICT

With unification, the elementary and secondary schools of most of western Contra Costa County (excluding only the small communities of Rodeo, Crockett, and Port Costa) were brought under a single administration. The boundaries of the RUSD run from the Berkeley city line at the southern edge, to Hercules on the north; from the San Francisco Bay on the west to the Oakland-Berkeley hills on the east. The district encompasses five cities (Richmond, El Cerrito, Pinole, Hercules, and San Pablo) and several unincorporated territories (Kensington, North Richmond, East Richmond, El Sobrante, Rollingwood, and Giant). (See map of RUSD, p. 27.)

Before unification each of the four elementary school districts comprising the RUSD had its own policy-making, administrative, and field staffs. Even tiny Sheldon, with only four schools, had its own board of education and superinten-

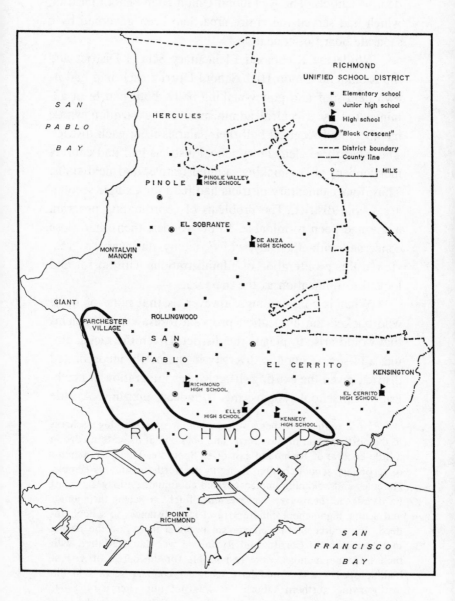

RICHMOND
UNIFIED SCHOOL DISTRICT

■ Elementary school
⊛ Junior high school
◢ High school
⬭ "Black Crescent"
-- District boundary
-·- County line

0   1 MILE

SAN
PABLO
BAY

HERCULES

PINOLE

PINOLE VALLEY
HIGH SCHOOL

EL SOBRANTE

DE ANZA
HIGH SCHOOL

MONTALVIN
MANOR

GIANT

PARCHESTER
VILLAGE

ROLLINGWOOD

SAN
PABLO

EL CERRITO

KENSINGTON

RICHMOND
HIGH SCHOOL

ELLS
HIGH SCHOOL

KENNEDY
HIGH SCHOOL

EL CERRITO
HIGH SCHOOL

R I C H M O N D

POINT
RICHMOND

SAN
FRANCISCO
BAY

dent of schools. The Richmond Union High School District, which had served the entire area, had been governed by a separate board of education.*

While the Richmond Elementary School District and the Richmond Union High School District each had had its own field staff and policy-making body, both had been administered by a central administrative organization whose members had received half their salaries from each district. The other three elementary school districts had had entirely independent policy-making, administrative, and field staffs. Thus, four elementary districts had fed into a single secondary school district. The problems of coordinating program alone had been formidable. Little wonder, then, that those concerned with efficiency, with economy, and with program viewed this proliferation of administrations with horror and looked to unification as the panacea.

What is confounding, however, is that none of those who backed the unification proposal foresaw the problems that would arise to plague the district. Given the racial, ethnic, and socioeconomic diversity in the newly incorporated district, given the existing struggle over integration in northern urban school systems, this is, indeed, puzzling. A little

* Before unification there were no junior or senior high schools in the northern end of the district and only one at its eastern edge in a little enclave of Richmond east of El Sobrante. Therefore, parents of secondary school children living in the northern suburbs (Pinole, Hercules and adjoining unincorporated communities) long ago must have resigned themselves, however unwillingly, to seeing their junior and senior high school children travel long distances to school. Indeed, one source of the antagonism between them and the people in Kensington, El Cerrito, and Richmond was that the latter, with their large populations, were responsible for the defeat of several bond proposals that would have located secondary schools in the fast growing northern suburbs. It was not until February 1964, eight months before the unification election, that voters in the high school district passed a bond issue that would result in the construction of a high school in Pinole and two junior highs, one in Pinole and the other in El Sobrante.

more than five years later, every respondent in this study — liberal or conservative, proponent or opponent of unification in 1964 — agreed that unification had been a mistake.

Whether that pessimistic judgment about unification is considered well founded depends upon the framework of values within which unification is viewed and upon whether one speaks of long run or short run gains. From the perspective of the upper-middle-class liberals, the short run results would seem disastrous; unification opened their schools to control by people they call "red-neck know-nothings" and dimmed what immediate hopes they had for an integrated school system. The working-class and lower-middle-class conservatives, on the other hand, see themselves in a constant struggle against domination by "ultra-liberals" who are brainwashing their children and encouraging them to abandon parental values, while threatening to inundate their schools with black children whose life style and values they abhor. But the long run impact of unification on such problem areas as integration, community control of the schools, or the quality of education is yet to be seen.

With reference to integration, white upper-middle-class supporters of unification from the south end of the district argue that if the district had not been unified, the old Richmond Elementary School District could have been desegregated with relative ease, since most of the white support for integration came from that sector. An alliance between the sophisticated, organization-wise whites of Kensington and the El Cerrito hills and a determined black community representing about 40 percent of the school population probably would have been able to override any opposition. But how much white support actually could have been mobilized to integrate schools with such a high proportion of black students is an open question.

Furthermore, even if integration could have taken place under those conditions, other long-range policy and ethical considerations must be taken into account. For example, without unification the suburban schools would have remained almost totally white, since those communities had no significant black population in residence. Since unification, however, some of these schools have been forced to open their doors to black students who have been transported from overcrowded, dominantly black central-city schools. What difference this will make in the education of black children or in the attitudes of the whites is not yet known, but for those who still believe that the solution to America's race problems lies ultimately in an opportunity structure that is open equally to blacks and whites (a dream that must start with equal schools) and in early and meaningful contact between the races, the situation holds a slim promise.

With reference to community control, some foresee an ultimate irony — an alliance between white conservatives and black militants in which demands for integration are dropped in return for support of community controlled schools. Richmond has not yet had very active black demands for community control, so the experiences there may not be applicable to other communities. What happened, however, does suggest that the conservatives may be willing to enter such an alliance only when the threat of integration is real and immediate and when they see no other way out, while that is the very situation in which the black community would be least responsive to such negotiations.

During the 1969 school board election campaign, spokesmen for the conservative, neighborhood schools forces approached the most articulate black advocate of community control with a deal: In return for his support in the election, they would support black demands for local control of their schools. The black leader declined the offer because he felt that the conservatives could not be trusted to keep their part of the bargain; he believed that, once in office, they would be unwilling to share either the power or the money that effective local control demands.

Shortly after the election in which the conservatives had taken over the school board, a delegation of prominent black leaders met with the board members-elect and offered to trade their promise not to push integration for some measure of decentralization and local control. Firmly in command, the conservatives replied, "No deal."

FINANCIAL CONSEQUENCES OF UNIFICATION

On the financial side, the promised economies never came to pass. Indeed, just as opponents had argued, unification resulted in decreased revenues, for of the four school districts involved, only Richmond had a substantial industrial tax base with which to support its schools.[4] The other three districts had all been classified by the state as "low wealth" districts,* and, as such, had been receiving substantial state aid at the time of the unification election. Once unified, Richmond's industrial and commercial wealth put the new district well above the low wealth category, and all

---

* A low wealth district is defined as one that has less than three-fourths of the state's average assessed valuation per pupil. For example, the average assessed valuation in the state in 1969 was $13,198. Therefore, a low wealth district in that year would have had $9,972 or less in assessed valuation per student.

It is one of the ironic inequities of school financing that middle-class suburban districts with relatively high per-capita income often fall into the low wealth classification because they lack industrial tax bases that would boost their assessed valuation, while the urban areas, with their heavier industrial tax bases, fail to qualify despite enormous demands made upon a city's tax dollar. Thus, for example, in 1968/1969 suburban Mt. Diablo Unified School District, a low wealth district, had a state income per average daily attendance (ADA) of $332, compared to Richmond's income per ADA of $252. The state's contribution to Mt. Diablo's general fund in that year was 49.8 percent; to Richmond's it was only 34.1 percent. This sort of imbalance in the distribution of state school funds is the target of court suits in several states, including California.

extra state aid ceased. The slim financial incentives offered for unification were more than offset by this loss. An informant who was then a member of the Richmond Elementary School Board, and an articulate advocate of unification, commented sadly on the financial outcome: "We were led astray by our professional experts. We really believed what we were told about the economy of the unified district."

In addition, the unification law requires that a newly unified school district's tax rate must produce revenue equal to, but not more than, the income derived from the tax rates of the component districts. Under this formula the tax rate for the new district came to $3.14, a figure that represented a tax decrease of $.61 for Sheldon and $.36 each for Pinole and San Pablo. Only Richmond suffered an increase of $.14. Richmond's wealth, which had been adequate to support the original, smaller district, was now spread very thin.

From the point of view of the state, unification had accomplished its economic purpose; the state was relieved of its financial obligations to three poor school districts. From the point of view of the local taxpayers, they were betrayed. The experts had promised economies, but had not said for whom. Now the people were expected to pick up a much larger proportion of the cost of running their schools from property taxes. Whatever joy might have existed in the Sheldon, Pinole, and San Pablo school districts because of their tax decreases was short-lived.

At the first business meeting of the new RUSD school board March 24, 1965, the superintendent of schools called the new board's attention to the major financial problems facing the district. Teachers had requested a substantial salary increase, and rising costs had made the maintenance of extant educational programs impossible at the existing income levels. Ironically, the special programs that the poorer districts had been able to afford because of the additional state aid they had received — music, language, enrichment, recreation, and the like — were among the first to be threatened with extinction.

Reluctantly, the new school board agreed to place a proposal for an increase in the tax rate before the electorate on June 29, 1965. This request for increased taxing prerogatives was soundly defeated in an election in which only about 16 percent (12,655) of the eligible voters cast ballots.* From this distance it is difficult to identify the causes of that defeat with certainty, but since one of the major selling points of unification had been economy, it is reasonable to speculate that those who bothered to vote were telling the new district that they expected that promise to be fulfilled.

Disappointed, but fearful of another rebuke, the board declined to make another attempt to increase the tax rate, arguing that even if the voters were to approve an increase after July 1 (the start of the district's fiscal year), it would not solve current problems because, according to law, no tax increase in a school district could become effective after the start of a fiscal year. Hence, if on July 15, 1965 the voters of a district agreed to increase their taxes, the increase could not be levied by the school board until July 1, 1966. For the next three years the board hedged on placing another tax rate increase proposal before the voters. Discussions about financial problems occur repeatedly in the minutes of board meetings, seeming always to culminate at the "wrong time" in the fiscal year.[5]

Meanwhile, educational programs were being curtailed; by 1969 summer sessions were sharply reduced, and there was talk of eliminating them entirely.[6] Special pro-

---

* Until the busing issue arose, elections pertaining to school matters, whether for school board trustees or for tax increases or bonds, stirred the voters very little; turnout was always very small.

grams not paid for totally by state or federal funds were eliminated, for example, Operation Headstart and school health programs. Class sizes crept up; maintenance standards slipped so far that by 1968 teachers, administrators, and the public agreed that they were endangering the health and safety of children. Teachers complained continually about a lack of books and supplies, and salaries failed to keep pace with those in comparable districts.[7] By the 1968/1969 school year salary schedules in the RUSD ranked twenty-fourth among twenty-five of the largest Bay Area school districts, having fallen from $527 above the Bay Area average in 1956/1957 to $243 below that average ten years later.[8] The school board and administration blamed the community for their failure to support their schools with their dollars; their opponents insisted that the district's plight was primarily due to the incompetence of those in control.

INTEGRATION

As I have indicated, unification presented significant new barriers to desegregating the elementary schools. While the political unit governing the schools was new, the area had a history of troubled race relations that dated back to World War II, when large numbers of blacks and southern whites were recruited and brought by segregated trainloads into Richmond to work in the shipyards.

Between 1941 and 1943 four Kaiser shipyards were built in Richmond, which at their peak employed 115,000 workers. Obviously, neither Richmond nor the surrounding area could supply this manpower; therefore, company recruiters scattered throughout the land to persuade families to relocate in Richmond. These efforts were particularly fruitful in the south and southwest, and tens of thousands of workers — black and white — were soon being brought into the city. One study of the workers at the yards showed that about half the newcomers, both black and white, came from Oklahoma, Arkansas, and Texas.[9] So great was the influx that in the three years between 1940 and 1943 the population jumped about 300 percent, from 23,642 (of whom just over 1 percent were black) to 93,738 (of whom 6 percent were black). By 1947, two years after the war, the count stood at 101,519 — of whom 14 percent were black, an increase in the black population of about 5,000 percent in the seven-year span.[10]

From the outset, relations between blacks and whites were tense and antagonistic. Obscenities such as "nigger," "jigaboo," or "zigaboo" were common.[11] Commenting on her observations, Kathleen Archibald wrote: "In most of the whites the hatred was basic, a deep-seated and strong flavored aversion that was evident in almost every gesture or remark. . . ."[12] In these circumstances, violence was imminent, always just below the surface.

In addition, the promise of northern "streets paved with gold" was not fulfilled for black workers who suffered severe discrimination on the job. Many of the craft unions at the shipyards had national constitutions that proscribed black membership. Since the yards operated under closed shop contracts, this effectively denied craft jobs to black workers. Moreover, both white employees and their supervisors thought of blacks as mentally and morally inferior, unfit for any but the most menial tasks. Consequently, blacks were kept out of supervisory positions, except on rare occasions when they would supervise all black crews; and they were not hired for office or white-collar positions. In sum, only the most menial and unskilled jobs fell to blacks.[13] Robert Wenkert summed it up neatly:

> Indeed, in every area possible the practice was to keep the Negro separate; when that was not possible, then to keep him "in his place." It turned out . . . that his "place" was on the bottom rungs of the social and economic ladder.[14]

The federally financed workers' housing projects were completely segregated. By the peak year of 1943, 60 percent of the population of Richmond was living in these jerry-built structures that lined both sides of Cutting Boulevard from just below San Pablo Avenue almost to the bay, a distance of about three miles. In 1950, 78 percent of Richmond's black population still lived in the projects.[15] During the war there were only two places in the city where black families could find housing — the black projects and North Richmond, a scantily populated shantytown that turned into a swamp with the first winter rain. Housing segregation in Richmond continues to be acute; the patterns that were established in those early war years still prevail.

Currently, most of the RUSD black population is segregated into what is known locally as the Black Crescent, a ghetto that runs along the entire western edge of Richmond and is separated from the main city by physical boundaries roughly paralleling the Eastshore Freeway, the Santa Fe railroad spur, the Southern Pacific tracks, and the Santa Fe mainline (see map of RUSD, p. 27). The Richmond extension of the Bay Area Rapid Transit system follows these railroad routes. Its proposed several foot high barrier, referred to by local critics as the BART Wall, will further increase the visibility of the separation between the ghetto and the rest of the city.

Soon after the war ended, suburban development began, and large numbers of whites moved out of the city. In the decade from 1950 to 1960, Richmond's population fell from 99,544 to 71,854, while the population of Western Contra Costa County (roughly the territory of the RUSD) remained relatively stable — 155,220 to 158,600 — indicating a large-scale internal migration, mostly of young white families from the central city to San Pablo, Pinole, and the burgeoning suburban areas of El Sobrante, Rollingwood, and Tara Hills — all now under the jurisdiction of the RUSD.[16] During the following decade, the total population of the city showed little change (79,043 in 1970), but the ratio of white to black changed significantly. The white population decreased by 8,638 (15.4 percent), while the black population increased by 14,145 (99 percent). Blacks in 1970 comprised just over 36 percent of Richmond's population compared to 20 percent in 1960; whites in 1970 were about 60 percent compared to 78 percent ten years before.

Complicating this tense racial situation and increasing the pressures toward conflict is the socioeconomic diversity in the area. On Richmond's north flank lies a group of communities that are dominantly white working-class and lower-middle-class, peopled by many who left the central city in order to escape the problems of living in a biracial community and the fears and tensions that smoldered just below the surface of city life. It is little wonder, then, that these white suburbanites resist having to confront the same problems again in their schools. Here, also, conservative politics, fundamentalist values, and a narrow construction of the meaning and function of education are strong. To the south, on the other hand, lies an area dominated by people holding the liberal, cosmopolitan, and integrationist world view of the professional upper-middle class, where a broad liberal arts education is valued as an end in itself, and which is the only white sector of the district where integration received substantial and articulate support.

In sum, state policy imposed unification on a heterogeneous area where community bonds were few and the sources of tensions many. It brought together three disparate populations — blacks, working-class and lower-middle-class whites, and upper-middle-class whites. The differences

between the whites and blacks need not detain us here since
this is a study of white behavior, but the differences in values, life styles, political commitments, and educational philosophy between the two groups of whites are so great that
reconciling or accommodating them would be a difficult
task, indeed.

CHAPTER **3** # WHITE AGAINST WHITE

I know what it's like to live in a tough neighborhood where the kids take turns beating you up every time you walk around a corner. I fought desperately to better myself and to get out of that neighborhood. Then all of a sudden they were talking about busing my children back there to the same school where I went. If they think they can do that to me, they're crazy*

Since the McCarthy phenomenon of the early 1950s many American social scientists have sought to understand what we have come to call the revolt of Middle America.[1] Notions of status politics,[2] the private-regarding nature of

---

* The thirty-one respondents represented on the following pages included the eleven men and women who have served as school board members since the unified district was organized, and the twenty leaders of the two major organizations on either side of the conflict

the working class,[3] and working-class authoritarianism[4] grew from that undertaking. While these concepts have gained wide currency in American intellectual thought, when applied empirically to the RUSD, they failed to offer a satisfactory explanation for the behavior of the working class and lower-middle class there.

STATUS POLITICS

The concept of status politics generally is best understood as standing in opposition to the notion of interest politics; the former is supposedly animated largely by status anxieties and resentments, and the latter by economic interest. In this context, status politics is seen as the irrational projections of the insecure, the frustrated, the uncertain upwardly mobile, or the displaced downwardly mobile; while interest politics is seen as the rational expression of group interest. From that reasoning, it follows that status politics is the expression of the ideological mass whose wide-ranging demands are impossible to attain, while interest politics is the expression of class or interest groups whose narrow demands are essentially economic.

Writing in 1965 to clarify his earlier formulation about status politics, Richard Hofstadter said:

> . . . the literature of the American right was a literature not of those who felt themselves to be in possession but of those who felt dispossessed — a literature of resentment, profoundly anti-establishment in its impulses. We were struck by . . . its profound hostility to the culture and institutions by which it was surrounded.[5]

This "profound hostility to the culture and institutions" that surrounded them is precisely what I saw among the conservative leaders in the RUSD, but they were neither upwardly mobile nor downwardly mobile, neither people of ethnic origin trying to prove their 110 percent Americanism nor native-born Americans clinging to vanishing positions of superiority. Only two families had ethnic backgrounds, and none could be characterized as downwardly mobile. To the extent that there has been upward mobility among them, it is probably more accurately described by Bennett Berger's concept of stratum mobility which, rather than presenting an image of large-scale upward mobility by *individual members* of the working class, suggests that in an extended period of affluence *a whole stratum collectively raises its standard of living.*[6]

The status-interest dichotomy attempts to separate economic interest from a group's interest in maintaining its life style and value system, when, in fact, those social conditions flow from its economic position. To separate them is to fail to comprehend or to give due weight to the impact of the economic condition on social life and on the development of values. In order to understand and interpret the hostility of the working class and lower-middle class, it is necessary to understand that it is directed at institutions that dominate their lives and over which they have little control. The working-class and lower-middle-class people in Richmond *felt* dispossessed because they *were* dispossessed, *both culturally and educationally.* They called for schools that would reinforce their values and life style, and they were heard with contempt by the upper-middle-class school board. They called for an education that would prepare their children for a life of hard and relatively unrewarding work, and they were called narrow and provincial.* Over and over, conservative leaders said that they were furious because the world was being run by "those liberals," because they were frightened that their children would be

---

* Many upper-middle-class liberals in the district argued that it was beneficial to society for those children to have an education that would broaden their horizons. While that may be true, it does not refute the facts as the conservatives saw them.

seduced by alien ideas that would ultimately separate them from the family. Such perceptions can be characterized as irrational projections only if one believes that there is a single culture in this land and that the major institutions serve every segment of the society equally well. The schools in Richmond do not. Whether in the quality of teachers, the physical plants, or in reading achievement levels, the children of the working class are shortchanged. From their perspective, integration would expose their children to still another set of alien values (those of the blacks) while offering them no incentive to take the risk, since there was no promise that any of these deficiencies would be alleviated.

Analysis of school achievement records in the RUSD shows that among white students reading scores are directly correlated with socioeconomic status (SES). The lower the SES, the lower the reading scores at all elementary grade levels — a finding that is not unique to the Richmond schools. Using an SES scale ranging from a high of 1.0 to a low of 8.0, Table 2 shows that among dominantly white schools, Kensington, the school with the highest SES in the the district, posted the highest median reading scores (94 percent, 92 percent, and 86 percent in Grades 1, 3, and 6, respectively). Tara Hills, a school in the middle ranges of the socioeconomic scale, showed median scores of 68 percent, 57 percent, and 54 percent in the same three grades, while Dover, at the lower end of the SES range, showed scores of 32 percent, 36 percent, and 37 percent.

Black schools in the district range from 4.7 to 6.0 on the socioeconomic scale, and reading achievement is substantially lower in them than at comparable white schools — a fact that was given wide circulation during the desegregation struggle — and many white parents were very angry about proposals that would integrate their children into schools with students who performed worse than their own, where the teachers were reputed to be less competent, and where the school plants were often quite dismal. Moreover, my working-class respondents were well aware that the children in the upper-middle-class hill schools performed academically much better than theirs did, and several seemed to accept that as part of the natural order of things. More than once I was told that they thought it quite natural that their children did not achieve as well as the children of "those professors and other people with lots of education up there on the hill." If that were indeed natural, then why, they asked quite logically, was it not natural that black children would perform even more poorly?

Table 2. Median Reading Scores in Selected
RUSD Elementary Schools, 1968[a]

SES[b]	Percent Black	School	Median Reading Scores		
			Grade 1	Grade 3	Grade 6
2.0	1%	Kensington	94%	92%	86%
4.3	0	Tara Hills	68	57	54
5.8	2	Dover	32	36	37
5.9	93	Nystrom[c]	35	28	14

SOURCE: *Compiled from Research Bulletin No. 17. State Test Results By Individual School for 1966, 1967, and 1968. A Technical Report of the Richmond Unified School District.* January 10, 1969.

[a] See Appendix, Table A1, for scores of all elementary schools in the district.

[b] See Appendix, Document 1, for Occupational Rating Scale used by the RUSD to establish school SES. The scale ranged from a high of 1.0 to a low of 8.0. No elementary school in the district was rated higher than 2.0; none was lower than 6.0.

[c] The reading scores for this dominantly black school are shown for comparison.

Through two election campaigns (1967 and 1969) and as often as they had an audience in between (at least twice a month at school board meetings) anti-integration leaders reminded the community that black schools had been characterized by the liberal school board as inadequate both physically and educationally. If that were true, they asked, why should their children be forced to attend them? At the same time, they hammered away at the relationship between SES and school achievement in the RUSD. They cited the Coleman Report to support their argument that the problem was socioeconomic status, not race, and gave wide publicity to that report's major conclusion that the most important variables related to school achievement were the family background of the child and the social class of the school.[7] Of course, they left out any mention of the report's finding that black children achieved better in integrated settings without deleterious effect on the whites.

Given their racial hostilities and fears, and given that they were quickly and persuasively informed that integration would provide no benefit to their children, it is hardly surprising that these lower-class parents resisted so tenaciously. And, indeed, if the hope of school desegregation is that it will make a difference in the school performance of black children, the integration of black and white working-class children — both of whom perform poorly — makes little academic sense.

In other ways, too, the schools of the white working class are little better than those of the blacks. Like the black schools, they were built long ago to accommodate relatively small central city populations. The city's population has grown tremendously, but the school sites remain the same, and there is no more room for expansion. Among them are some of the least attractive and most crowded plants in the district.*

Finally, if we agree that there is a relationship between the classroom teacher's experience and the quality of teaching, then both blacks and poor whites are cheated (although the whites still fare better than the blacks), for there is a

* See Appendix, Table A2, for comparisons between the sizes of central city and suburban school sites.

close correlation between the socioeconomic status of a school's population and the number of inexperienced teachers (as judged by probationary status) in that school. Table 3 shows a summary picture for a sample of twenty-seven schools — the nine dominantly black schools, nine white schools drawn from the upper half of the SES scale, and nine white schools from the lower half. The relationship is quite clear: the lower the SES, the higher the number of probationary teachers.

Table 3. Relationship Between School Socio-economic Status (SES) and Percentage of Probationary Teachers in Sample RUSD Schools, 1970–1971

SES[a]	Number of Teachers	Number of Probationers	Percent of Probationers
White Schools			
2.0–4.0	160	46	24
4.1–6.0	175	76	43
Black Schools			
4.7–6.0[b]	208	132	63

SOURCE: Richmond Unified School District, 1970/1971.

[a] On a scale ranging from a high of 1.0 to a low of 8.0, no school ranked higher than 2.0; none was lower than 6.0.

[b] The SES of the nine black schools ranges from 4.7–6.0.

Given these realities, is it more reasonable to look for status anxieties and resentments to explain the political mobilization of the working class and lower-middle class, or to suggest that their experience had taught them to suspect that there would be little benefit for their children in the proposed integration program?

"PUBLIC-REGARDING" *vs.* "PRIVATE-REGARDING"

Social scientists have long been concerned with differences in life style and ethos between the middle class, the working class, and the poor and with the way those differences affect both public and private behavior.[8] The condi-

tion of the lower strata of our society has been variously
attributed to their inability to defer gratification [9] or to the
fact that poverty is debilitating and develops a culture that
ultimately reinforces the deprived state. [10] Edward Banfield
and James Wilson's [11] notion that private-regarding and
public-regarding behavior can be explained with reference
to class-cultural differences is in the tradition of that general
body of research.

Most likely to be public-regarding, according to Wilson are "citizens who rank high in income, education, or
both" and who consequently have "an enlarged view of the
community and a sense of obligation toward it." These are
people who "have a propensity for looking at and making
policy for the community as a whole." [12]

The private-regarding, on the other hand, are likely
to be poor, relatively uneducated, lacking in the experiences
and the "skills [necessary] for participation in organized en-
deavors," and attached only to organizations that "are in
some sense extensions of the family and the church." [13]
These people are likely to be mobilized to collective action
only "when each person can see a danger to him or to his
family in some proposed change; collective action is a way,
not of defining and implementing some broad program for
the benefit of all, but of giving force to individual objections
by adding them together in a collective protest." [14]

Reflecting upon that definition, it seemed to me that
the common good for which the public-regarding elites al-
legedly are willing to sacrifice too often is coincident with
elite good to be an artifact of chance. Melvin Tumin, too,
casts doubt on elite claims that they act in the public interest, characterizing them as "patent nonsense" and indicative
of the "power of self-deception." He writes:

> In the face of these claims, one cannot help but reflect that
> if we were to believe all the people, groups and nations who
> assert that they are doing things only out of the best of mo-

tives and solely on behalf of the interest of others, we should find ourselves in a world dominated by fanatically altruistic and selfless people, living out their lives only to see to it that others should be able to enjoy the good life.[15]

And, in fact, inspection of the RUSD integration plan shows that the upper-middle-class children were to be integrated into Martin Luther King School, the only ghetto school that had a brand new plant, that was being developed as a demonstration school with a specially selected staff, and that already had several federally funded special projects offering academic enrichment and innovation, and where more were promised.* These plans made the integration program palatable for the upper-middle class; they could foresee an immediate payoff. I quote from one interview at length since it tells the story most compellingly.

I: Why did you support two-way busing?

R: I supported it because I believe in integrated schools as being good for all kids ultimately and good for education. I was bused as a child all my life in what people would consider very unsafe conditions — that is, in Middle Western winters — and we were bused home for lunch, too, so we rode the bus four times a day. So I don't have the fears.

---

* This school was so favored for two reasons. First, its new plant was built because the old neighborhood school failed to meet state earthquake-safety standards. Second, since it included among its students the children of many of Richmond's middle-class black families, it qualified for few compensatory education funds. Yet students at King fared almost as badly on standardized tests as did those at Verde (whose record is the worst in the district), so their middle-class parents have exerted continuing pressure on the administration for improvement and the district has poured in funds from other federal sources. Its new plant, coupled with all the special projects, made it an ideal choice for a district showplace — proof that black children were not discriminated against — and a school to which the academically oriented upper-middle class would not object to sending their children.

I: Were you concerned about the possibility that academic standards would be lowered?

R: It was my impression that King school would not be one bit less academically oriented than Kensington.

I: Well, then would you have been willing to send your child to Verde?

R: [Emphatically] No! I'm not willing to experiment with my children. They have only one chance to get educated.

I: Then how could you have taken the position that the Broadway and Dover [white working-class schools in San Pablo] parents should send their children there?

R: [*She hesitated, reddened with confused embarrassment, and finally spoke lamely.*] Well, I mean I wouldn't send my child to Verde if it were 97 percent black and with such poor facilities. But if I felt that under the plan the school had potential, that would be different. [*Then, very defensively*] I was willing to send my child to an integrated school; those people down there weren't even willing.

These observations suggest that the most important thing to be said about the public-regarding/private-regarding conceptualization is that it is both irrelevant and misleading. Misleading, not because one can find no truth at all in it — education may make a person better able to perceive long run benefits at the risk of short run costs — but because it never touches the more important reality that only the affluent can afford the short run costs. Irrelevant, because in the real world the educated and the affluent elite are rarely called upon to pay any serious costs — a situation that seemed obvious in the RUSD and which James Wilson aptly, if unintentionally, demonstrated in his study of the urban redevelopment program in the Hyde Park-Kenwood district of Chicago.[16] Examining that situation, he concluded that it was the private-regarding ethos of the poor blacks who were to be displaced by the redevelopment plan that disabled them from accepting — no, favoring — their removal as necessary to the best interest of the larger community. Their public-regarding brothers, "upper-middle-class professors, housewives, and business and professional men," who made the renewal decisions that would deprive poor blacks of their homes, Wilson assures us, were acting only for the benefit of the whole community and, sadly enough, went unappreciated for their trouble.

I am not clear whether Wilson would have us believe that it was happenstance that the common good was identical with the elite good — that is, low income blacks were moved out of that middle-class neighborhood, thereby stabilizing property values and keeping the neighborhood intact — but the notion of the common good applied here does stretch credibility, and one can hardly blame the displaced blacks if they did not believe it.

WORKING-CLASS AUTHORITARIANISM

In his widely read chapter on working-class authoritarianism, Seymour Martin Lipset argues that the anti-democratic predispositions of the working class stem from the fact that they are concerned with the immediately perceivable, with the personal and the concrete (note the congruence with the notion of private-regarding), have a short time perspective, cannot defer gratifications, cannot deal with abstractions, and are unable to perceive complex possibilities and consequences of action.[17] These qualities, he concludes, make them especially vulnerable to mobilization in extremist and anti-democratic causes, and provide the basis for working-class authoritarianism.

Applied to the movement in process in the RUSD, this analytic construct proved deficient for several reasons. First, concern with the here and now is a rational response to life's realities among lower-class people rather than an impairment of either cognitive functions or imagination as is implied by the theorists of working-class authoritarianism. In order for planning to be meaningful, life must be predictable, and too often that is not the case among the insecure working class.

Second, the working-class people I was observing and talking with seemed to understand the consequences of their actions quite well. Rather, their failure to act in ways that were consonant with the upper-middle-class intellectuals' definition of democracy stems at least in part from the fact that they simply do not value or understand abstract notions of democracy as do members of the upper-middle class. Those of the working class are more inclined to look at the real world and ask, "What do those fancy words mean?" When they did so in the RUSD, they found that their children were not getting a fair break in the schools, and that those who were most facile with the rhetoric of democracy were uninterested in the beliefs and values of working-class people or in the problems of their children.

Third, notions of working-class authoritarianism explain nothing about *why* people suddenly become mobilized. The most we can say is that there exists an authoritarian potential among all segments of the population and that differences in education, life style, and values probably affect that potential more in some groups than in others. But that does not address the critical question: What activates that potential? The answer is not to be found in abstractions divorced from both the objective conditions of life and the concrete political realities that people confront. Rather, it is to be found by examining the relevant political issues and the way the people involved in them perceive those issues as a threat. Thus, when an American insists that communists ought to be barred from speaking on college campuses, it makes more sense to look at the political reality and the life situation from which that judgment flows than to speculate about his authoritarian personality. He lives in a world divided into two hostile camps, one labeled capitalist and democratic and embodying — he has been taught with a suffocating uniformity — all that is good; the other labeled communist and authoritarian and embodying all that is evil. At home and at school he has learned that communism is a destructive and subversive philosophy that must be resisted at all costs. His government spends the greatest portion of his tax contribution to maintain a system of defense to protect him from that enemy. If he has never gone to a college or university (as have all the upper-middle-class liberals in this study) where some attempt generally has been made to put the "grays" back into life, to examine these and other dogma critically, he has little basis for challenging the received doctrines. Seen in that context, is his answer a psychological aberration or a reasonable response to a lifetime of indoctrination?

In sum, my argument is that theories of status politics, working-class authoritarianism, and the private-regarding nature of the working class are fraught with the bias of their middle-class intellectual originators and that they have little explanatory force when tested in the empirical world. Instead, the analysis that follows suggests that more compelling explanations for political behavior are to be found in an examination of the political issue that evokes that behavior; in the social situation of the actors — that is, the objective conditions of their lives and their place in the social structure; in their hopes, dreams, and fears, which also generally are born of their place in the social system; in the social and ideological superstructure that prepares the way for political behavior; and in the guides for action that are implicit in their ideological commitments.

The protagonists in this struggle occupy different places in the social structure; that is, the conservative opponents of desegregation are largely working class and lower-middle class, while the liberal proponents are largely professional middle and upper-middle class. That means that they do different kinds of work, have different levels of education and different educational experiences, and hold different places in the power and status hierarchies of the society. These differences lead to disparate orientations to political issues, to work, to the meaning and purpose of education, and to the family unit, which, in turn, condition their hopes, their fears, and their aspirations, and set the course of their collision once the issues became salient. The rest of this chapter seeks to explain their behavior by understanding these social structural differences.

EDUCATION AND EDUCATIONAL PHILOSOPHY

When we look at the disparity in educational background and experience between the two groups of leaders, it hardly comes as a surprise that they have divergent expectations of the schools and define their ideal educational systems in wholly different terms.[18]

Median years of education among the conservative leaders is 13; among the liberals it is 18. Only three conservatives are college graduates, while fifteen of the sixteen liberals have at least a bachelor's degree and of those, nine have advanced degrees (see Table 4). The exception is the

Table 4. Levels of Education of Liberal and
Conservative Leaders, 1970

Education	Liberals	Conservatives
High School	1	12
B.A. or B.S.	6	2
Graduate or Professional Degree	9	1
TOTAL	16	15

lone black man on the executive board of the integrationist organization who has only a fifth grade education. Several of the liberals with B.A.'s are close to the master's degree;

one has completed all the requirements except the dissertation for the Ph.D. On the other hand, only one of the conservatives with a high school education has a degree from a two-year college; five others have had a year or so, usually at a junior college.

When a conservative is asked what he ideally expects from an educational system, the first phrases that almost invariably spring to his lips are "the three Rs," "more discipline in the classroom," "end sex education," and "get rid of sensitivity training and of liberal teachers who are trying to brainwash my kids." They want a no-frills, no-nonsense education, schools that will train their children to be moral and upright citizens, teach them to be patriotic, "put some starch in their spines," and avoid filling their heads with notions that parents do not understand. A conservative board member put it this way during one of the many debates about sex education: "The parents can answer any questions the children have, and what they can't answer there's no need for the kids to know."

The remark met with lusty approval from his large, sympathetic constituency in the audience. Another respondent, her voice filled with indignation and fear, said, "Do you know, they're trying to put the Hilda Taba Method in the schools!" "What's that?" I asked. "Let me tell you," she replied, her voice rising, "that's dangerous business and subversive, too. She's a colored woman [untrue] who developed this method of teaching by *concept and inquiry* that they use to brainwash our children."

Responding to the same question about their ideal expectations of an educational system, the liberals answer that they want schools that will encourage "spontaneity," "innovativeness," "initiative," "flexibility," "independence," and, above all, that will not stifle "the natural curiosity and creativity with which children come to school."

There was no point at which the responses merged or

even came closer together. While these differences drive from a complex background including parental values and educational status, they probably are also a response to the work experiences of the two sets of parents. Most of the liberals in this study are professionals whose work allows them great freedom and requires innovation, independence, and initiative. Expecting that their children will follow in their footsteps they call for an education that encourages those qualities above all else. But of what use would those qualities be to a factory worker, a clerk, or a petty bureau-crat — the lot of most of the conservatives — where the con-ditions of work are largely unfree, monotonous, and repe-titious, and where a free spirit probably would endanger the job? Such dull, routine jobs may require more than anything else a kind of iron self-discipline just to get to work every day. If so, then most of those holding those jobs could be expected to wish for a disciplined child rather than an innovative one, since they probably have little ability to imagine the requirements of a work situation that is free.[19]

Parenthetically, it is interesting that in their emphasis on basic skill training and discipline in the classroom, the lower-class whites seem to have more in common with blacks than blacks do with their upper-middle-class allies — a discovery that came as no small surprise and disappoint-ment to some of the integrationist whites, as the following comment illustrates.*

> We tried to start a school after the new [conservative] board
> was elected, an integrated private school, but it became clear
> very quickly that the black parents wanted very different

---

* See Michael B. Katz "The Present Movement in Educational Reform," for a discussion of the differences in educational philosophy between the upper-middle class and the poor. Katz emphasizes the naïveté of the upper-middle class and argues that their failure to perceive and appreciate those differences is due to the "romantic fantasy" which is "at the core of much educational radicalism."

things from a school than we did. We had to give up the idea. It's ironic that they really want the same things from the schools as the people in San Pablo.

Ironic perhaps, but to be expected, since the schools fail their children in the same way. The difference is in degree, not in kind.

Consonant with the educational philosophy they expressed, not a single liberal spontaneously indicated that he thought the schools should focus more on teaching the basic skills. When I asked why, they would often shrug carelessly and say that they were not worried about their children's learning to read or write; they took that for granted.* And that is an apt assumption, for, by and large, their children did read well and attended schools which showed the highest reading test scores in the district.

On the other hand, one of the primary demands of the conservatives is that the schools place more emphasis on the three Rs, a response to the fact that the schools their children attend do not place well on standardized tests.

OCCUPATION, INCOME, AND THE HIGH COST OF LIVING

The occupational picture of the two groups reflects their educational differences. Using standard census categories, Table 5 compares the occupations of liberals and conservatives. Notice that thirteen of sixteen liberals are professionals, while only two of the fifteen conservatives fall into that category. One liberal leader— the only black man — is a blue-collar worker, compared to nine conservatives.

Among the liberal professionals, occupational stability is remarkably high. There has been almost no occupational

---

* As the discussion proceeded, they did indicate some concern that many high school graduates were functionally illiterate, and a few did speak of the need for better training in basic skills, but it was ˙ apparently of no immediate concern. They were interested in other, and to them more important, educational matters.

change and very little job change since they finished school.
Median job tenure is 10.5 years.

Table 5. Occupational Classification of Liberal and Conservative Men.[a]

Occupational Classification	Liberals	Conservatives
Professional, Technical, and Kindred	13	2
Managers, Officials, and Proprietors (except farm)	2	2
Clerical and Kindred	0	4
Sales Workers	0	2
Craftsmen, Foremen, and Kindred	0	3
Operatives and Kindred	1	2
TOTAL	16	15

[a] Where the respondent was a woman, the husband's occupation
was considered.

Among the conservatives, job changes are considerably more frequent; median years on the current job is 4.8.
Although as a group they are younger than the liberals by
5.5 years (median age of the conservatives is 36 years, of
the liberals, 41.5), the difference is not enough to offset the
significant differences in occupational and job stability,
which make the conservatives considerably less secure
economically.

As would be expected, income differences are equally
striking. Table 6 shows that the modal income among liberal families in the study is over $25,000; among conserva-
tives it is between $10,000 and $14,000. Ten of the liberals

Table 6. Annual Incomes of Liberal and
Conservative Leaders

Annual Income	Liberals	Conservatives
More than $25,000	6	3
$20,000–24,000	4	0
$15,000–19,000	5	4
$10,000–14,000	1	8
TOTAL	16	15

earn over $20,000, while only three conservatives do; all three of those were members of the school board at the time of this study. But the differences are more profound than these figures would indicate, for, with the exception of the one black man in the $10,000 to $14,000 bracket and one widow, all the liberals who earn less than $25,000 a year are young professionals who have not yet reached the peak of their earning potential. Among the conservatives, on the other hand, most are at or close to the peak of their expected lifetime earning curves and can expect only such increments in earnings as will come from cost-of-living increases or union negotiation.

When considered in conjunction with the fact that these are largely young families, the importance of the last point cannot be overestimated. In their middle thirties, these working-class and lower-middle-class men reach their maximum earning potential at the very stage in the family life cycle when pressures for spendable income escalate — that is, when the number of children at home is highest, when housing needs are most pressing, when household consumer durables become necessities rather than luxuries, and when the wife is least able to leave the home to help. To cope with the squeeze, these men may moonlight or work overtime,[20] they may live in a state of helpless outrage and frustration over the high cost of living and taxation; or they may do both.[21]

Thus, the conservative school board and its constituency attack the Work Incentive Program, a state sponsored program to encourage high school-aged girls who are welfare mothers to complete their graduation requirements, which allows each student up to seventy-five dollars for such expenses as graduation announcements, class rings, and college admissions applications. And liberals who earn $20,000 and more each year shout "racist." While racist feelings probably are one factor motivating the conservative attack on this program, there are other objective factors that are equally important. Consider that these hard working people regularly must make choices among comforts and have relatively few luxuries. Mainly in the $10,000 to $14,000 income bracket, with an average of almost three children per family, they struggle to feed their families and to keep up the mortgage payments on modest homes.* Those with older children either cannot afford to supply the expensive high school graduation amenities or do so at considerable sacrifice to family needs. As they see it, the taxes they pay buy privileges for others which they cannot afford for themselves. Not much of a bargain, they conclude. That some of their rage is displaced onto blacks — the handiest scapegoat in American life — should be no surprise.

EDUCATIONAL ASPIRATIONS

The differences in occupation, income, and education between the two groups lead to differences in the ways both parents and children perceive school and value education, and in their aspirations for the future.

Every upper-middle-class liberal parent in this study aspired to some form of higher education for his children, and, while no doubt those parents were concerned about their children's ability to make a living, that was not central. More than anything else, they talked about wanting their children to do what "would make them happy" or "would offer them fulfillment," and there was an implicit assumption that without education that goal could not be achieved. Thus, education was valued not for instrumental purposes, but as an end in itself.

---

* One respondent, a teamster earning almost $14,000 a year, complained bitterly: "I'm no better off than I was when I was earning $9,000 a year. Every raise I get just seems to make us come out the same, what with prices going up all the time. We used to eat steak oftener when I was making less money. My wife says we can't afford it now."

The working-class and lower-middle-class conservative families were much more ambivalent about higher education.* The five who said unequivocally that they saw a college education in their children's future were vocationally oriented and referred only to their sons; only one talked about learning in some broader sense as the goal of a college education.

EDUCATION FOR WOMEN?

While it is hardly news that boys and girls are subjected to different socialization processes and role expectations within the family, it was surprising to find how sharp the differences were between classes in attitudes toward women and their role. When talking about educational aspirations for their children, it never occurred to the upper-middle-class parents to leave their daughters out, while it rarely occurred to a working-class mother or father to include a daughter. Thus, whatever the aspirations of the professional middle class for higher education, they included both sons

---

* These observations are only tentative since the sample was small and unrepresentative. Nevertheless, it is interesting that they contradict many other studies which suggest that, regardless of class, most people aspire to college educations for their children. Some speculations about that disparity are in order: 1. If the question is closed, people may say "yes" because they think it is expected, whereas if they are permitted to talk freely, some of their ambivalences surface. 2. Other samples may have had larger ethnic populations, and ethnicity probably makes some difference in educational aspiration. In fact, the only two families of ethnic background in this study were both unequivocal about wanting their children to go to college. 3. This study took place at the height of campus turmoil and in a community adjoining the University of California at Berkeley. The fears these respondents felt about rebellion on the campuses were clearly expressed; several explicitly said they would never permit their children to go to Berkeley. It may be, therefore, that their ambivalence toward college in general was connected to those fears generated by the events on campuses at that time.

and daughters at least through the college level. But the only working-class father who talked about wanting his daughters to go to college said it was important because "in college they can meet a better type man who can support them better." Even that, however, was an advanced view. Most others would agree with a conservative school board member who said: "For my girls, they don't need to go to college. I want most of all for them to get married and have homes of their own. I want them to be first of all good wives and mothers." These views are congruent with the differences in education and status of the women in the families of the two groups and with the range of alternative roles each group permits to its women.

The conservative women had substantially less education than their liberal counterparts— a median of 12 years compared to 16. Of the sixteen liberal families, thirteen women had at least bachelor's degrees; only two had no college at all. Conversely, of the fifteen conservative families, only one woman had a college degree; only four more had had a few months to a year of college, usually at the local junior college.

The conservative women married younger — with a median age of 19 years at marriage, compared to 23 among the liberals— and were considerably younger when they bore their first child. There is an average of 1.2 years between marriage and the birth of the first child in the conservative families, 3.2 years among the liberals.

While most women in both groups were housewives, the proportions differed substantially — 80 percent among the conservatives and 56 percent among the liberals.* Of the seven liberal women who were employed, five were professionals and two were secretarial workers, while of the three conservative women employed, only one was a profes-

---

* Since these percentages are based on a small number (15 conservatives, 16 liberals), they must be viewed as suggestive only.

sional — a teacher — and the other two were part-time secretarial or clerical workers.

Nevertheless, the recent ferment among women had made itself felt in both classes. A question about the occupation of the women of the household was met with defensive reactions from both liberals and conservatives, men and women. On the upper-middle-class liberal side, it took the form of an almost shamefaced discomfort over the need to reply "housewife." The women generally shifted uncomfortably in their seats, lowered their eyes, and muttered the word. A few rushed to assure me that it was "only until the children get a little older" and presented some evidence of preparation for that future day. Their husbands seemed almost equally discomfited by the question and almost always volunteered some information about the professional status of their wives before their children were born. One man answered, "housewife, liberated."

On the working-class and lower-middle-class conservative side, however, with few exceptions the women seemed to draw themselves up to their full heights, to sit straighter, and to respond clearly, "housewife." One young woman took the opportunity to express her outrage at the women's rights movement.

> I'm a housewife, and that's my most important job. I'm very down on professional women with families. Women have hurt men a lot, although the man was at fault in the beginning to let them get that toehold in. I hate the Women's Liberation Front. I think it should be a man's world.

While most did not go that far, several others volunteered the information that they were "proud of my job," "doing the most important job there is," "wouldn't be anything else." And their husbands agreed. "I wouldn't have it any other way. What kind of man would I be if I couldn't support my family," was one typical comment. And another,

"I don't believe in career women. My wife hasn't ever worked in the eleven years we've been married."

This vehement response in support of a traditional role for women— so out of tune with the times, with my own experiences, with the large literature on the discontent of modern American women, and with the fact that one-third of the work force is made up of women — was deeply puzzling. I could understand the value that a working-class family placed on the financial ability to allow the mother to stay at home; to have both parents out of the home when there are young children and where adequate child care is not available can be catastrophic to the family. Moreover, women of the working class who are also in the labor force generally have the doubtful privilege of doing two full days work in one — one on the job and the other after they get home at night — a way of life that few women would choose. Thus, for the working-class or lower-middle-class wife to be able to afford to stay at home is a valued advantage and a significant step up.

But the anxiety about role and status seemed to be an expression of more than those rather ordinary things, and none of the replies sounded very convincing. Rather, they had the air of extreme defensive reactions, fearful responses to the erosion of traditional values. It was as if by reaffirming those values more loudly, by clinging to them more tightly, they could keep the world from changing before their eyes.

But what, my reader may ask, does this discussion of women's role in the family have to do with the conflict over school integration? The answer, I suggest, is that the difference in the way the woman's role is defined in the two groups contributes to different family responses on the question of neighborhood schools.

The professional upper-middle-class family represented here values independence among all its members and encourages them to seek to maximize personal development.[22] Thus, even though in a very limited way, women are expected to orient to a world outside the family. The choice of a professional career may be difficult for a woman in this stratum, but it is no longer unthinkable among large segments of that population. The result: a woman is not solely dependent for validation upon her role within the family; ancillary roles are legitimately available to her. Therefore, she does not desperately need to make motherhood and housewifery a full time career in order to justify her existence.

The working-class and lower-middle-class subculture, on the other hand, is dominated by an inner-family orientation; members are expected to find both social and emotional gratifications within its bosom. No woman worthy of the title *Mother* would wish to do otherwise. In fact, it is she who is counted the failure if some member of the family turns outward for fulfillment of his or her needs. In such a family, nurturing it and raising the children become a woman's only meaningful functions. The result: the child-centered family and the family-centered role of women become mutually reinforcing. Take any part of that job away prematurely and the woman will fight like a tiger, not, as is often thought, to protect her little ones, but rather to preserve for herself as long as possible the only legitimate role identity that her social world permits.

The difference in attitudes toward nursery school between the two groups lends some support to these speculations. While most children of the professional upper-middle class attend nursery school, none of the working class and few of the lower-middle-class children have any nursery school experience. Because of my own upper-middle-class bias, I assumed at first that this was because the cost would have been a financial burden for the working-class families, but as I talked to family after family, it became clear that

the reasons were more closely related to family role definitions than to finances. (After all, the difference in the annual income of a teamster who makes about $14,000 a
year and an associate professor at the university is not great.)
With that realization, I began to ask my conservative respondents why they did not send their children to nursery
school. The almost unanimous reply was that young children belonged at home with their mothers, that "they get
sent out into the world young enough, and we should be
willing to protect them as long as possible." Quite aware of
the disparity between her own beliefs about nursery school
and those of the upper-middle class, one working-class
mother remarked:

> We know our children are going to have to grow up, but we're
> not going to push them out of the nest because we're too lazy
> to take care of them like those people up there in the hills.

Ironically, then, the notion that "woman's place is in
the home" may have unintended social consequences, for it
seems possible that it is one of the structural sources of the
conflict when the needs of school integration call for busing
children from their neighborhood schools.*

LOCALITY

The class differences I have been discussing mean that
the participants in the struggle live in quite different neighborhoods — the upper-middle class in the hills; the working
class and lower-middle class in the flatlands, closer to the
black ghetto. It is to be expected that opposition to integration will be more virulent and more violent in fringe neigh-

---

* Cf. Richard Sennett, *Families Against the City*, where he argues
that the inner-family orientation among lower-middle-class families
of late-nineteenth-century Chicago retarded upward mobility among
their children. Also see Herbert J. Gans, *The Urban Villagers*, where
he contends that the "person-orientation" of Italian-Americans and
their concomitant peer group commitments inhibit upward mobility.

borhoods where interracial exposure exists because both groups are too poor and too powerless to avoid it and where, as a consequence, contacts are more likely to be abrasive and to provoke hostility.

Robert Dentler and Constance Elkins offer evidence that prejudice is highest in "naturally unsegregated" schools — that is, schools in fringe neighborhoods — as compared with schools that are "planfully desegregated."[23] The reason, they argue, is that naturally unsegregated schools are located in those neighborhoods undergoing the most rapid ethnic residential change, and their very location in a racial fringe area may cause both blacks and whites to perceive them as undesirable. Michael Rogin, too, argues that prejudice against blacks, as expressed in support of George Wallace's bid for the presidency, was activated by proximity and visibility.[24] The large and active black population in Gary, Indiana triggered whites' fears so that they voted heavily for Wallace, while comparable white ethnic minorities in Milwaukee, Wisconsin, where the black population was relatively small and inactive, failed to support him.

The anti-integration leadership in Richmond largely lived in such fringe neighborhoods or had only recently escaped them.* Several respondents spoke with great feeling about their struggle to escape those neighborhoods, and all insisted that they would never send their children back.

In contrast, most of the district's upper-middle-class proponents of integration lived in a quiet, peaceful hills area, high above the turmoil of Richmond's black ghetto. The few blacks who were their neighbors shared their middle-class values and life style. They hardly ever saw a ghetto black; the menace of a ghetto rising was an abstraction far

---

* Most of the conservative leaders lived in or near San Pablo, a small, working-class city adjoining the North Richmond ghetto, where 54 percent of the population earned less than $8,000 a year in 1968.

from home; and the specter of their children being ac-
costed, perhaps beaten, by a band of angry black youths
had little reality in their lives.

RATIONALITY AND IRRATIONALITY

Until now I have argued for the rationality of the conservative position; from their perspective, self-interest demanded opposition to integration. For members of the lower
classes, life is a fierce, competitive struggle with a zero-sum
system of rewards; that is, if you win, I lose. That reality
and the threat it poses enables people to deny certain facts
before their eyes — for example, that racial discrimination
exists — and to blame the victim's debased condition on
some inherent failing of his own. It facilitates the "I'm-not-
prejudiced-I-just-think-people-ought-to-earn-their-keep" response. For after all, to open their unions to blacks is to
threaten the jobs of whites. And since, if given the chance,
the majority of blacks in America would be competing with
the craftsmen, the clerks, the petty white collar workers, and
the semi-skilled workers who were my respondents, from
their perspective it makes sense — at least in the short run —
to try to keep them out. It is their jobs, their neighborhoods,
their schools that are the most immediately threatened.

But there is also a profound irrationality in the single-
mindedness of the position of these working-class and lower-
middle-class people. They vehemently attack any program
of assistance for the black poor, but quiescently accept the
public policy that dispenses favors to the already well-
favored — charity in the form of tax loopholes, subsidies to
private, profit-making industries, construction of roads and
highways for the benefit of private industrial development,
and the like.

I wondered, for example, why my conservative respondents were not demanding free medical care for themselves,
rather than wishing to deny it to those who were poorer.

Since that matter came up spontaneously very often, I asked about it. The answers were an aggregate of nonrational notions related to the American creed of individualism and personal achievement:

> I don't need any help; I'll make it on my own.
>
> This country was built on every person pulling himself up by his bootstraps.
>
> What kind of man would I be if I couldn't take care of my family?

When I replied that the government not only helped the poor but the rich as well, and pointed out that Standard Oil (the most important industry in the district) was "helped" through such devices as oil depletion allowances, most said that that was all right with them. After all, "Standard supplies a lot of jobs around here, don't they? They oughtta get some breaks. S'pose they went out of business, then what would we do?"

If we think in terms of the Marxian notion of false consciousness — that state of consciousness in which people, responding to the ideological and social superstructure that surrounds them, are no longer able to perceive their own self-interest, let alone to act upon it — both the conservative anger at benefits to those who were worse off than they and their passivity and acquiescence in the face of far greater benefits to those who were better off become comprehensible. The system had taught them to believe in a highly individualistic notion of achievement, assuring them that each man got his just rewards. Why, then, should somebody get something for nothing? For those who have to run so hard just to stay in the same place, it must be especially galling. On the other hand, they have also been taught that without the American corporate structure the country would fall upon evil times. Thus, in their own interests, the people must sacrifice to protect those corporations. "S'pose they went out of business, then what would we do?" So, they accept the subsidy of aircraft manufacture as part of the national interest, and when, in the midst of rising unemployment and spiraling inflation, the President offers a program of tax relief to industry in lieu of programs directed at alleviating some of the most immediate pain of the unemployed, that seems right and natural — especially to those who are not yet unemployed.

Is it any wonder that these working-class and lower-middle-class people who are caught in so many binds are so angry and so ambivalent, that they displace their hostility downward and scapegoat blacks? They have yet failed to make the connection that the appropriate target of that anger is not those poor people whose misfortunes are greater than their own, but a social system that breeds such inequities and whose ideology so distracts its citizens that they are unable to perceive them.

RACIAL STEREOTYPES AND THE POWER OF PRECONCEPTIONS

Since it is impossible to live in a racist society without absorbing some of those attitudes, both liberals and conservatives hold racist attitudes and beliefs. But there are sharp differences in the behavior and attitudes of the two groups. The liberal integrationists acknowledge that America is a racist society and that whites have discriminated unjustly against blacks for centuries; the conservative anti-integrationists do not. The liberals are aware that they have been complicit in these injustices, and they wish to redress them; the conservatives disagree. The liberals struggle against negative stereotypes and irrational fears; the conservatives do not admit their existence. Among the conservatives, racism is gross and obvious; among the liberals, it is subtle and more difficult to detect.

For example, despite the evidence to the contrary,[25]

most of those who said they were committed integrationists could not shake the fear that the presence of black children in the classroom would diminish educational quality, a fear that made their commitment to integration very ambivalent. They wanted integrated schools but, as one parent said, "My children only have one chance to get educated, and I'll not sacrifice that." These were after all, the upper-middle-class intelligentsia of the district, people who prodded their children to high achievement levels and who, by and large, expected them to qualify for elite colleges and universities across the country. The emphasis for them was on quality education. Anything less was unthinkable, and they were really not certain that integration did not mean less.

And while the integrationist board members can be justly proud that when they had the opportunity they appointed the first (and to this date, the only) black man to serve on the RUSD board, what they chose to tell me about him was curious, indeed. For after informing me that he was a lawyer and a graduate of "fine Eastern schools," each in turn presented this black man's family background as if giving me a dog's pedigree. Each in his own way told me that he came from a "fine family of lawyers and judges," that there was a "long line of educated professionals in his background," and that his wife was also "a cultured and educated person"; in short, he was "an unusual man with an unusual background, a real find." Moreover, the minutes of the public meeting at which the appointment was announced show one board member making the public statement that "Mr. Hatter's parents both are university graduates and practicing attorneys and all four grandparents are university graduates who completed graduate work." [26] It was as if his parents were somehow meaningful in evaluating the adequacy of their choice for his performance as a board member. "Look," they seemed to be saying, "we didn't appoint just any ordinary nigger." When I asked whether the board members knew anything about their other colleagues' families, one respondent looked surprised and said, "Why no. I don't think so — at least I don't." *

Since racial fears and stereotypes were more prevalent, more overt, and more gross among the conservatives, distorted perceptions and projections of their own feelings and anxieties were more common among them. They generally refused to admit that white society had any responsibility for the plight of the blacks. They granted that "we have a problem," but it stemmed, they said, from the fact that "the colored just can't seem to get along." Nothing stood in the way of blacks but their own deficiencies, these working-class and lower-middle-class respondents insisted. If black children did not do well in school, they argued, it was only because their parents did not value education, because they were undisciplined, and because they did not "talk proper English" — the last being said very forcefully by a man who, in another context, assured me that "We haven't went to forced two-way busing, and we've made great strides."

Indeed, it is one of the ironic observations of this study that the very people who mistreat the English language most are the quickest to criticize the language and dialect of blacks. One reason they resist sending their children to ghetto schools, they insist, is that black children speak so poorly. Yet the language deficiencies among their own

---

* Several people who read this manuscript before publication argued that this was not a valid illustration of racism. After all, they said, those board members knew they risked stirring up racist criticisms when they appointed a black man. It was quite reasonable that they should assure the community about his qualifications, since "most blacks are poor and uneducated." When I reminded them that whites were, also, and that these board members never had felt the need to offer such reassurances about a white colleague, they looked startled. By their own argument they documented my point that racist perceptions among the upper-middle-class intelligentsia are subtle, indeed.

friends and colleagues go unheeded. When one of their number argued that he ought to be free to send his children to
any school he chose, just so long as "it's credentiated" and
another said, "I always have spoke my mind," they apparently were unaware that anything was wrong with their language. It leads one to wonder whether the very perception
of language inferiority is related to the fact that the words
(or dialect, or cadence, or all three) are coming from a person whose skin is black. A newspaper story from Beaumont,
Mississippi which desegregated its schools in the fall of
1970 summed up the point with a delicious irony. A white
woman came up to the school principal on the first day of
classes to ask whether her fourth-grade daughter would
have a black teacher:

> You know, they speak different from what we do. So it ain't
> that I'm complaining. It's just that I would like a white person
> to teach my daughter English.[27]

Reflecting their racial fears and tensions, these conservative whites are inclined systematically to overestimate
the proportion of blacks in the community and in the schools.
Thus, although in the city of Richmond the black population in 1970 was just over 36 percent, several conservative
respondents put it at well over 50 percent. One suggested
that it was as high as 80 percent; another offered his view
that the nearby Berkeley school system was refusing to di-
vulge the proportion of black students there because it was
"now up to 75 percent or 80 percent because so many white
families moved since they put in that busing plan." In fact,
black students in the Richmond schools represented 27 percent of the school population; and in Berkeley about 45
percent were black, a figure that had remained relatively
stable through the previous three years.

These observations are not new, nor are the people of
Richmond unique. In 1954, Robin Williams and Margaret

Ryan observed the same phenomenon in Cairo, Illinois where, despite official census figures showing that the black population never exceeded one-third of the total, the belief persisted among white residents that blacks made up one-half to three-quarters of the city's population.[28] More recently, Reginald Damerell, writing of a desegregation struggle in Teaneck, New Jersey, also documented the stereotyping of blacks.[29] There, where the blacks were all very substantial middle-class families. Teaneck whites saw them as "slum dwelling and culturally deprived." And there, where the elementary school that was 50 percent black had higher achievement scores than three white schools in a district of eight schools, adherents of neighborhood schools insisted that integration would diminish educational quality.

Finally, probably because they are more prejudiced on matters of race, there is a greater tendency among the conservatives than among liberals to project their own feelings onto external events, distorting the events to make them fit their beliefs. One of their most tenaciously held beliefs is that most black parents do not favor busing. By way of documenting that conviction, several people told me that the black, pro-busing candidate in 1969 had not carried the precincts in the black community. Said one of the leaders of the anti-busing campaign:

> You know, one of the things that amazed us most was that Reverend Smith ran so poorly. We figured that he'd take 65 percent or 70 percent of the vote, but he didn't even do that well in the colored precincts. Why in some of those precincts, he didn't even take 50 percent of the vote . . . . And all those whites who were so hot for busing didn't even vote for him. Why he ran last of all their candidates.

The reality is that district-wide he ran second of the three integration candidates, a slim 122 votes behind the front-runner. He carried every black precinct in the district overwhelmingly, by well over 86 percent, and led his white running mates in those precincts by 316 and 568 votes respectively. But the presentation of these facts did not change their beliefs. Instead, I was told by seven people with whom I discussed this that I was mistaken. One man went so far as to say, "I know you're wrong because I checked those returns out myself."

This, then, is a sketch of the two groups that squared off to fight the battle of integration in the Richmond schools. Given their different places in the social system and the different perspectives that derived therefrom, it is little wonder that they were unable to talk to each other in ways that would facilitate cooperation, if not understanding. While the upper-middle-class liberals had some ambivalence about the impact of integration on their schools, both their place in the system and their belief in their ability to control their own fate gave them some assurance that they could make whatever school their children attended a good one. And they probably were right. Conversely, the conservatives also probably were right when they felt less secure about their children's fate under the plan to integrate and less sure that they could influence that plan or their children's destiny. For the lower-class conservatives, the threat — both real and imagined — was immediate and palpable, any pay-off so distant as to be unimaginable. Is it any wonder that the battle was so violent and so filled with hatred that no one is likely to recover soon?

PART THREE

THE BATTLE IS JOINED

CHAPTER **4** **THE SEEDS OF DISHARMONY**

My family brought me here when I was two when they came to work in the shipyards. I lived in Harbor Gate; y'know, the white housing project for shipyard workers. I just don't understand. When the federal government brought us up here and built those houses, they built one tract for whites and one for blacks. *They* built the segregated housing, and then they come along a few years later and call *us* racists.

While the controversies over financing the schools and over the divergent educational philosophies of the two groups were rooted in important structural and ideological differences, they were fed by the battle over integration. Indeed, that was the key issue around which thousands of people were mobilized. Without the integration struggle the other issues would have lain largely dormant as they had for years, in part because, as several conservatives admitted, it had never occurred to them that they had the potential to take over the district. Once organized, however, they found that an important and vocal minority of their anti-integration constituency could be rallied around the other issues, and their goals were quickly reordered. The purpose then became not just to stop integration, but to capture the district so that they could implement their own educational philosophy.

SEGREGATED SCHOOLS

In Richmond, as in other urban areas across the country, segregated housing means segregated schools. I do not mean to suggest, however, that there is an accidental relationship between the two, for both Richmond's black ghetto and its segregated schools are the result of a long history of deliberate public policy.

Segregated housing was supported there by local, state, and national law, and, in this instance, was directly financed by the federal government. Given the concept of neighborhood schools that has dominated American educational policy, segregated schools naturally flowed from there. But in addition to the "natural" consequences of housing segregation, schools in Richmond were kept segregated either through the selection of sites for new buildings or through the manipulation of school attendance boundaries.*

As far back as 1947, the San Pablo Elementary School District, which then served children living in the North

---

* That racism is an old phenomenon in the Richmond schools is aptly illustrated by this story told by one district administrator: "When I first came here [as a teacher] in the early 1950s, racism was open and rampant. I even saw one teacher who punished white kids in the classroom by surrounding him with black kids and saying 'There, y'all can just stay with them for a week and see how you like it. Maybe that'll teach you to behave.' The district is still stuck with many of those teachers because they're in tenured positions. Until they reach retirement, there's not much hope of real change in the classrooms."

Richmond ghetto, built the Verde School to accommodate those black children. In 1955 their plan to build a second elementary school in North Richmond was met with strong opposition because the school would have been as segregated as Verde.

Richmond's record was little better. In 1958 the National Association for the Advancement of Colored People (NAACP) complained to the school board:

> The worst example of boundary location is the predominantly "white" Downer Junior High School. Negro children living within a few blocks of Downer are being transported much longer distances to other schools, while white children are being transported even further distances to Downer.

Nor are these isolated instances from the past. In 1967, when the liberal board was still in power, an optional attendance area was established between the Belding School (whose black population was then 4 percent) and Peres School (with a 93 percent black population), which carved a three block strip right out of the Peres attendance area and permitted those children to go to Belding.[1] It is surely more than coincidental that those three blocks were an island of white in a sea of black.[2]

The first major controversy over school integration occurred in 1958/1959 before unification, when the Richmond Union High School District integrated the secondary schools through the relatively simple expedient of redrawing their attendance boundaries.

In the RUSD, as in the rest of the San Francisco Bay area, affluence increases as you move uphill — not an exact correlation, but a close approximation. Thus, residential stratification in the RUSD runs from the flatlands on the west to the hills on the east. The equation is roughly: the higher the altitude (or the closer to the heights), the higher the socioeconomic status. Recall that most of the district's blacks are confined to the Black Crescent on its flat, western edge. Obviously, then, if secondary school boundaries ran in a north-south direction, as they did before 1959, those schools were effectively stratified both by race and by socioeconomic status. After redistricting, each high school attendance area ran in an east-west direction, from the hills to the bay, assuring some schools a better racial and socioeconomic mix, although by no means one reflecting the population distribution. But given the patterns of residential stratification, no amount of tinkering with boundaries would assure a more balanced population in all schools. Richmond High, for example, lies close to the border between white Richmond and San Pablo, both dominantly working-class communities, both with more than their fair share of poverty.* To assure Richmond High a larger proportion of students from affluent families, some students would have had to be brought in from distant sectors of the district, while some students living near the school would have had to be sent elsewhere. Similarly, short of moving large numbers of students around, there was no way that Kennedy or Ells High Schools, both located on the edge of the black ghetto, could have had anything but very large black populations (see Map of RUSD, p. 27).

Nevertheless, even such changes, which would have

---

* Richmond is primarily an industrial city; about three-fifths of its employed men are manual workers. In 1965, 15 percent of the white men and 37 percent of the black men in Richmond were unskilled workers. (Alan B. Wilson, *Western Contra Costa County Population, 1965. Demographic Characteristics.*) Similarly, San Pablo is described by its senior planner as a "small blue-collar community without any industry." As of 1968, 38 percent of its population was in the $3,000 to $8,000 annual income bracket; 16 percent earned less than $3,000. Thus, more than half the population in this city of about 20,000 inhabitants, of whom only about 4 percent were black, earned less than $8,000 a year. Poverty in San Pablo, therefore, is almost exclusively white. (See Appendix, Table A3, for a more detailed comparison.)

affected only students in secondary schools, were greeted with strife which culminated in an unsuccessful move to recall four school board members.[3] The controversy over integrating the secondary schools, where students ranged in age from 13 to 18, tends to cast doubt upon the argument heard in the crisis over elementary school integration that opposition was directly related to the tender ages of the children involved — that is, that such small children must be kept in their neighborhood schools, close to home. For those who remember the secondary school integration dispute recall that at that time high school students were also defined as "small children."

In 1970 the district had forty-eight elementary and thirteen secondary schools (seven junior high and six high schools) attended by 41,191 students (23,309 in elementary schools and 17,314 in secondary schools). In 1966 white Anglo students accounted for 68.2 percent of the total, blacks for 22.6 percent. Table 7 specifies the details for the years 1966 to 1970. Note the steadily rising fraction of black enrollment and the decreasing white enrollment, a change due not to a significant increase in the number of black students but to a decrease in the number of whites.*

There are eight elementary schools inside Richmond's

Table 7. Racial Distribution of Students in
the RUSD, 1966–1970

Race	1966	1967	1968	1969	1970
Anglo White	68.2%	67.9%	66.9%	65.2%	63.4%
Black	22.6	23.3	24.2	25.7	27.1
Spanish-speaking White	5.6	5.2	5.2	5.3	5.5
Other	3.6	3.6	3.7	3.9	4.0
TOTAL	43,782	43,872	43,123	41,367	41,191

SOURCE: Richmond Unified School District.

* The number of black pupils in RUSD schools in the years from 1967 to 1970 was respectively: 10,122; 10,424; 10,615; 11,170. In the same years whites numbered 29,859; 28,860; 26,960; 26,097.

Black Crescent, and a ninth one lies just on its periphery. In 1967 these nine schools accounted for 87 percent of the entire black student population in the district. Table 8 indicates that there has been some dispersion of black students from these schools during the four years between 1967 and 1970. Partly as a result of a school board decision in 1968 to bus black children to alleviate overcrowding in ghetto schools, partly because of an open enrollment plan instituted in 1969, and partly because blacks were slowly moving into what were formerly all white neighborhoods, in 1970 the schools in the ghetto accounted for only 64 percent of the black elementary school population.

Table 8. Percentage of Black Students in
RUSD Elementary Schools and in the Nine
Ghetto Schools, 1967–1970

Year	Blacks as Percentage of All Elementary Schools	Percent of all Blacks in Ghetto Schools
1967	24%	87%
1968	25	79
1969	26	69
1970	27	64

SOURCE: Computed from statistics published by the Richmond Unified School District.

Table 9, on the other hand, shows the percentage of black students in the nine ghetto schools for the years 1967 and 1970. Notice that while the absolute numbers of children in those schools decreased by almost one-third, the proportion of blacks generally either remained the same or rose slightly in the four-year period as the few white children have left. Thus, these schools are becoming more segregated with time.

Given the location of these schools, there seems to be no way to integrate them with respect to both race and socioeconomic status without some fairly long bus rides. Indeed, so concentrated is the ghetto in Richmond and so removed from the rest of the city, that even to integrate with neighboring schools — an unsatisfactory solution, since it would mean sacrificing socioeconomic balance and integrating working-class and poor blacks with whites of the same class — would require the transportation of children. This is the price that housing segregation exacts.

Table 9. Blacks as a Percent of Students in
Nine Ghetto Elementary Schools,
1967 and 1970

	1967		1970	
School	Number of Students	Percent Black	Number of Students	Percent Black
Coronado	816	98%	525	98%
Cortez	554	74	398	93
Lake	590	37	451	35
Lincoln	578	46	436	54
King	864	93	691	94
Nystrom	848	93	695	96
Peres	1,176	93	746	93
Stege	617	81	482	78
Verde	595	98	332	99
TOTAL	6,638	82%	4,756	84%

SOURCE: Computed from statistics published by the Richmond Unified School District.

THE RUSD'S FIRST SCHOOL BOARD

Shortly after the unification proposal passed, a special election was held to select the five members who would serve on the newly unified school board. School board members are elected at-large rather than as representatives of a specific sector of the district, a practice that often effectively disfranchises significant portions of the population. In the Richmond schools, for example, no black or Chicano has ever been elected to the board; * only one working-class per-

* One black man, an attorney, was appointed in 1966 to fill the unexpired term of a member who resigned. He served barely a year, failing in his reelection bid in 1967.

son served between 1945 and 1970; and, as we shall see, the political composition of the board has too often been homogeneous, its character depending on which side has been most successful in mobilizing its constituency.

The first RUSD school board was no exception. Elected from a field of nineteen were two women, both civic leaders who had served on the boards of several community and county agencies, and three men, two of whom were high-ranking executives of Standard Oil and one of whom was a professor at the university. Three of the five earned well over $25,000 a year; a fourth earned close to that; and the fifth was a widow living on a pension and savings. All were college educated. One had been just a few units short of a master's degree before leaving school; one had a master's degree; and two had doctoral degrees. Four of the five had been serving on one of the two Richmond school boards before unification; the fifth had served on the board of one of the other districts.

Consonant with their upper-middle-class incomes and education, four of the five lived in distinctly upper-middle-class neighborhoods. Three owned homes in Kensington; one lived in Point Richmond (which houses most of Richmond's small upper-middle-class) but identified with what he described, straight-faced and without a touch of irony or self-consciousness, as "those high-minded Kensington types who are filled with civic virtue and integrity." The fifth lived out near El Sobrante, but he also was oriented by way of income, occupation, education, life style, and values to the south-enders in Kensington and the El Cerrito hills.

Thus, the north end of the district, that sector where conservatism was strongest, was without geographic or political representation on the new board. Instead, the board reflected the moderate-liberal coalition that had grown up in the wake of post-Sputnik public concern over the performance of the schools.* Two were liberal Democrats; three were moderate Republicans. Today all but one of the Republicans describe themselves as liberals; all are more in tune with liberal Democratic opinion than with the Republican party to which they remain registered. Their relationship to that party may best have been described by one of their number, who said, "I remain Republican because I think some of us who think as I do ought to be Republicans."

These, then, are the five men and women who would try to govern the district — an educated, sophisticated, cosmopolitan, upper-middle-class elite; moderates by both temperament and social position who were supported by many who would soon become their enemies. Committed to the notion that politics was the art of persuasion, convinced that rational discourse was the way to bring about change, they soon found themselves buffeted by a tempest of emotionalism in which rationality was all but obliterated.

THE DIVISIONS SURFACE

The new RUSD board had its first organizational meeting March 16, 1965. The first few meetings after that were preoccupied with the major problems attendant upon unification — adjusting salary schedules for maximum uniformity, assessing the financial condition of the district, prepar-

---

* In addition to the national trauma engendered by Sputnik during the late fifties, the Richmond schools were experiencing important changes in the composition of their population. The black population continued to grow as a fraction of the total, not only because of a steady in-migration of black families, but because of an equally steady out-migration of white families from central Richmond. At the same time, the expansion of university facilities in Berkeley brought an influx of university-related families, many of whom settled in Kensington and the El Cerrito hills. Starting in 1957, the white newcomers forged a moderate-liberal coalition which successfully placed some candidates on the elementary and secondary school boards.

ing the first budget. Nevertheless, even during this initial phase, the divisions began to surface.

On the financial side, the district faced immediate problems. After levying the available override taxes, there was not enough money to satisfy the demands of program, staff, maintenance, and supplies. Teacher and public dissatisfaction grew as the demands of each had to be compromised in the interest of economy.

At the same time, the Congress of Racial Equality (CORE) was agitating to do away with segregation in the schools. Within a few months CORE formally requested that the board acknowledge that *de facto* segregation existed in the schools and that it appoint a lay committee to study the matter and bring in recommendations for correcting the racial imbalance. The board agreed, and at its next meeting the president announced the appointment of a Citizens Advisory Committee on De Facto Segregation (CACDFS), saying that "the board had tried to provide a balance of race, sex and geographical distribution."[4] But there was no serious attempt to balance the committee politically, a fact that the conservative anti-integrationists played up very successfully in their attempts to mobilize the community. In fact, one of the prime movers in the early organization of the conservative community in the district said that he was galvanized into action by the appointment of that committee.

> I was shaken up by the appointment of that committee. I didn't know much about what was going on in the schools at the time, but I read about that in the paper, and I felt that the committee was not objective, but committed to a particular policy in advance.

Three board members agreed that this had been the case. A typical comment was, "Yes, I suppose it was made up of people sympathetic to integration, but there were many disagreements about how it was to be done. We took our resolution to mean that we meant to deal with desegregating the schools, so there was no point in appointing those who opposed integration." A fourth could not remember how the selections were made; and the fifth said, "We did try to involve people who were unsympathetic, but they all refused." * All agreed, however, that the appointment of the committee was a public acknowledgment that the schools in the district were segregated and that the board intended to remedy the situation.

It is this crucial difference in their basic premises that led to an irreconcilable conflict between integration and anti-integration forces. The liberal school board *assumed a policy in existence*, that is, that the district was committed to desegregating its elementary schools. From that perspective the committee's mission would not be to discuss whether, but *how*, and it made sense in that context that it was composed of people favorable to that policy. For the conservative opposition, however, *defining the policy* was the issue. The board could not legitimately establish policy without their participation, they argued. From that perspective, the committee would be expected to discuss *if* the schools were in fact segregated and *if* the school board had some responsibility in that matter.

In conversation with the board members who were responsible for activating CACDFS, it became clear that they expected this committee to be the vehicle through which they would gain community support for integration and through which the anti-integrationists could be persuaded to support their plans. Yet, they never sought to involve those people in any meaningful way in the study or

---

* Since at the time those who opposed the committee had no organization within which to caucus and wherein the political benefits of their refusal to serve could have been made clear (in fact, most were still unknown to each other), it is hard to believe that no one of the opposition could be found to serve on the committee.

in the discussion of the problem. When confronted with that fact, they all argued that it would have stymied the work of the committee to have included opponents of integration on it since they would have wanted to discuss *if* instead of *how* — an argument that is undoubtedly true. But if they understood that crucial difference in their underlying premises, what made the liberals think some magical conversion would occur? The answer, I believe, lay in their hope that, having legitimized the study of *de facto* segregation in the schools by appointing the committee, somehow their opponents would accept as binding the "law" that would flow from it — a hope that was justified by experience showing that such political performances generally do work to dampen the force of the opposition. One former board member explained it thus:

> We felt that the force of the law, the authority of the courts, the heritage of adherence to law was strong enough so that most people would go along — with strong regrets, but would go along.

Unfortunately, they failed to comprehend that this issue had evoked unusually strong feelings that would not be quieted through the traditional political mechanisms.

Finally, perhaps exacerbated by the frustration over the incipient struggle over integration and the faltering economic situation, other problems, indicative of the differences in educational philosophy, boiled to the surface. For example, an organization from the north end of the district, Parents for Educational Decency, protested the use of certain books in the English department at De Anza High School, which, they alleged, "contained four-letter words." * The group asked the board to state explicitly that such books, as well as those "containing things offensive to the Christian

* Among the books at issue were Richard Wright's *Black Boy* and J. D. Salinger's *Catcher in the Rye*.

religion or other religions, but to the Christian religion in particular, must be left out."⁵ Furthermore, they asked that parents be given a veto over books being used in the classroom, not only for their own children but for all children.

Contrary to these demands, the board adopted a policy that left the selection of books to the teachers in the individual departments in each school, taking care to ensure collegial checks on the literary and educational value of all suggested readings. But for the Parents for Educational Decency questions of literary and educational value were not of central concern, nor could they and the school board members have agreed upon the definitions of those values. The question for them was a moral one; they believed that their children were being corrupted by exposure to books "describing prostitution, incest, sex perversion,"⁶ and the board offered them no protection.

In sum, within five months after the unified school district board was constituted, the problems that would rend the district were clearly outlined: a financial bind that the voters were unwilling to alleviate; the differing educational philosophies that divided the educated, cosmopolitan upper-middle class from the morally restrictive, fundamentalist-leaning working class and lower-middle class; and the need to cope with a restive black community that was demanding an end to segregated schools.

CHAPTER **THE LIBERAL DILEMMA**

y early 1966 the lines of battle were being drawn — the white, professional upper-middle-class liberals who were at the helm *versus* the working class and lower-middle class who were angry, frustrated, and feeling dispossessed; the liberals ideologically committed to integration, the conservatives standing opposed; the liberals acting out the forms of democratic participation, the conservatives shouting "fraud."

THE CONSERVATIVES BEGIN TO MOBILIZE

The appointment of the Citizens Advisory Committee on De Facto Segregation (CACDFS) activated the latent fears of the anti-integrationists and set them in motion, but at first they did not know where to turn, how to proceed. The problem was soon solved for them when the school board ordered CACDFS to hold a series of public meetings, ostensibly to hear public testimony and sentiment, but in reality to legitimate the process of desegregation — an instructive illustration of what Herbert Gans has called the "performing government."

> . . . government must develop institutional means to shield itself from the citizens. In Levittown (and I suspect everywhere else) it does so by creating two governments, a *performing* and an *actual* one. The government with which the decision-makers confront the citizens is a performing government; its actions are *performances* that follow altruistic democratic theory. The stage, designed according to this theory and legitimated by state and local statutes, is the public meeting of the governing body, where decision-makers listen to citizens' opinions and then appear to vote on a final decision on the basis of what they have heard. But this is only a performance, for the decision has already been made "backstage," in the secret deliberations of the actual government.[1]

Those hearings and the people who planned them ultimately must bear the major portion of the responsibility for the quick and successful organization of the conservative anti-integrationists in the district,* for those who were soon to become leaders of the neighborhood schools forces report that before the first committee meeting they had felt isolated. They knew, they said, that there was substantial support for their position, but they did not know how to tap it. They were timid about speaking up because they were uncomfortably aware that they would be tagged as racists — a designation so unpopular and thought to be so politically disreputable that even overt racists would avoid it.

The first open meeting of CACDFS changed all that. For

---

* One former board member vigorously, if retrospectively, affirmed that judgment. "It was a great political blunder. Integration was simply too unpopular a cause, and the establishment of the committee provided the issue around which the anti-integration people could mobilize."

the first time, the conservatives found kindred souls from other parts of the districts with whom they could unite — people who were interested enough to attend that meeting and some who were bold enough to stand up and be heard there. Racial hostilities were barely concealed. One informant claims to have heard a woman shout angrily, "They're getting their foot in the door." One man who was soon to be elected to the school board complained bitterly, "Why does a minority group want to shove everything down our throats?" [2]

When the committee gave little evidence of sympathy for their viewpoint, the conservatives charged that the whole procedure was a meaningless charade and set out to communicate their anger and fears to their friends and neighbors. While no responsible authority in the district had ever yet mentioned busing, the word was spread that Richmond was about to emulate its Berkeley neighbor and institute a two-way busing plan. Because of the proximity to Berkeley, because at every turn someone knew — or claimed to know — some Berkeley child who had suffered a terrible trauma since busing had been instituted there, busing was a specter that could be exploited effectively. By the second meeting two weeks later, there were more than four hundred people present (compared to about one hundred and seventy-five at the first meeting), and the roster of conservative speakers was long and their supporters loud. By the time of the last open hearing a few weeks later, about a thousand angry people jammed the room, most of them opposed to any plan for desegregating the schools.

The publicity convinced many who had been paying little attention to the schools that something important was afoot and that they might not like what was about to happen. At the same time, the public debate helped to give legitimacy to the expression of latent racial prejudice and anti-integration feelings in the community. It became easier to acknowledge and to articulate one's own opposition when others were shouting it at every meeting and organizing to defeat integration proposals in every part of the district. One of the conservative leaders neatly summed up the role of the CACDFS in the conservative mobilization:

> After awhile the De Facto Segregation Committee started to hold public hearings. I went to that first meeting at Walter Helms [school], and I spoke up. Others who believed as I did also spoke up. In this way we found each other and were able to be in touch. We started calling each other right away and very soon after, the Citizens Committee for Neighborhood Schools [CCNS] was formed.*

In fact, CCNS was organized, incorporated, and made its first public appearance within one month after the first CACDFS hearing, and the conservative counterattack was under way. Two months later they presented the board with a petition containing about 11,000 signatures, which called upon the district to foreswear any intention of busing children for the purpose of racial balance.† The board refused

---

* While the movement in Richmond, as elsewhere, focused on the importance of the neighborhood school, when asked whether the quality or location of the schools had influenced their decision to buy their homes, of the thirty-one respondents in this study, only six said they had investigated both. Three others said they knew only what the real-estate agents told them. Of those nine, all but two said that the information about the schools had influenced their decision but was not the major factor. The house was the determining factor in the purchase decision, they said. The remaining twenty-two respondents said either that they had not thought about the schools or had been only minimally concerned when making the purchase. This confirms the findings of Carl Werthman, et al., in *Planning and the Purchase Decision: Why People Buy in Planned Communities*. They show that the quality of the neighborhood school is not a central factor in the decision to purchase a house.

† In March 1966 a racial disturbance in Richmond that grew out of an interracial fight among a few Richmond High School students had greatly agitated the community. Emotions had run so high that Richmond's police chief issued an order to "shoot all looters," an

to accept the petition, saying that public policy could not be made by petition, a position that enraged the CCNS leadership at the time and which still fills them with bitter anger. The superintendent and one of the board members did meet with the group's leaders privately some time later, but they were unable to reach an accord. One conservative explained why:

> We found out then that there was no way we could get any satisfaction whatsoever. Mrs. Berry kept assuring us that there would be no busing, but she never was able to tell us how she planned to integrate the schools without it, so we knew we couldn't believe her.

Neither Margaret Berry — a board member who favored integration — nor anyone else could tell them how the district could integrate without busing because, as the conservatives correctly perceived, no widespread integration was possible without transporting children.

THE SCHOOL BOARD BECOMES IMMOBILIZED

Action and reaction followed one another in a swift and escalating spiral. The very "performance" that the liberal board had counted on to cool out community discontent served, instead, as a mobilizing vehicle for the discontented. As talk about integration grew, so did the number of organizations in the community, both pro- and anti-integration. CCNS continued to appear regularly before the school board to make its position on the sanctity of the neighborhood school ever more firmly known.* Smaller or-

---

action approved and defended by many citizens. (See Robert Wenkert, et al., *Two Weeks of Racial Crisis in Richmond, California*, for a detailed account.) It is likely that this incident greatly facilitated the collection of signatures on the anti-busing petition.

* In 1970, when the same people who earlier had insisted that the principle of neighborhood schools was inviolate were on the school board, they cut off kindergarten enrollment in seventeen ele-

ganizations and parents associations, largely composed of people opposed to any change in school attendance boundaries that might result in a better racial balance in the schools, sprang to life all over the district. At the same time, the black community, led by CORE, continued to present desegregation demands to the board, and white integrationists were beginning to stir. The board was quickly immobilized by these pressures.

One might ask what these policy-makers could have done to alleviate the bind in which they found themselves. The answer, I think, is nothing, as long as they were unwilling to enter a dialogue about *whether* the schools should be desegregated and as long as they were at the same time committed to acting out the form of democratic procedures without the substance.

Politically, they had two effective choices. One was to have structured CACDFS so that it would have been representative of the differences in the district and then resigned themselves to a long process of education. But with a black community pressuring heavily for action on school integration, it would have been politically difficult for the board to have appointed a committee that would have debated the issue interminably.

The other alternative was to have drawn and implemented an integration program without public discussion and fanfare and gambled that, when faced with a *fait accompli*, the people would have accepted the change with relatively little disorder. Had the board done so, the new program would have been in effect for months before the

mentary schools as an economy measure. Thus, kindergartners had to attend schools outside their neighborhoods. When questioned, the conservative board members insisted that this was consistent with their position that every child had an unassailable right to go to his neighborhood school. After all, they explained, parents were not being *forced* to send their children outside the neighborhood because kindergarten attendance was not compulsory.

opposition could have mobilized its forces for a counterattack. By then, the fears, the anxieties, and the forebodings (which were exacerbated by the months and years of discussion and the backing and filling of the school board) might have been allayed sufficiently to defuse the situation. (About this, more will be said in Chapter 11.) But for the liberal board members to have acted so forthrightly would have required an unambivalent commitment to integration, a supportive liberal constituency, and the political philosophy to support such firm action. The liberal board had none of these.

The fact that a white supports integration does not mean that he is free of negative racial stereotypes and fears. He takes his stand on integration because the American *ideology* has taught him that "all men are created equal" and that, therefore, all are entitled to equal opportunities and equal justice. At the same time, the American *reality* has taught him that, at best, it is only white men who are "created equal," and generations of discrimination against blacks have kept them in demeaned positions in the society, thus reinforcing the myth of black inferiority. Caught between the ideal and the real, the liberals' commitment to integration in the RUSD was deeply ambivalent. Ideologically they were convinced that equality of opportunity was not possible if black children attended segregated schools. At the same time, they were not really sure that critics who argued that integration would dilute the quality of education in their children's classroom were wrong. Given that uncertainty, the question was: what would they be willing to sacrifice? If by integrating the schools their own children would suffer academic deprivation and would be less qualified to compete for entrance into the best colleges and universities in the country, these people who valued academic achievement so highly would have to decide which value was more important — integration or Harvard. For the professional upper-middle class it was a tough choice, and one that most never made.

Their own ambivalence and the equivocal position of their liberal constituency made the board members very unsure, and they sought ways to reassure the liberals in order to prevent the erosion of their support. Indeed, the superintendent is reported by one of his lieutenants to have openly calculated that the liberal hills people could be seduced into supporting the integration plan by the promise that their children would be sent to the brand new Martin Luther King School. But the working class and lower-middle class were offered no incentives that might have made integration more attractive.

Throughout the years of listening to presentations from both sides, the board gave almost no indication of what integration policies it would pursue, no clue to how it would answer the questions that were on everyone's mind. Given the patterns of residential segregation, how could the district integrate and still retain the neighborhood school concept? Did integration really mean busing white children to schools inside the black ghetto? Was Richmond to become the next Berkeley? *

Each time the questions were put to them the board members reassured the community that it was not their intention to engage in mass busing for the purpose of school integration. "This district," one member said publicly, "will not go the way of Berkeley." Indeed, as late as January

---

* Early in the dispute, the black community indicated a willingness to accept one-way busing in which only black children would be bused to white schools. But most whites were unready to accept that compromise. Immobilized by the growing opposition, the board failed to act in that direction, and, if it ever could have worked, the moment passed quickly. By 1968 many whites, seeing the handwriting on the wall, were ready to accept black children into their schools, but by then the blacks were insisting that they would accept nothing less than two-way busing.

1968, the dominantly liberal board took a formal policy position *against* the busing of pupils. But when they were pushed to indicate how Richmond would integrate its schools, they hedged; and each time they did so, anxieties and tempers heightened because everyone knew that any serious district-wide integration plan would have to rely on busing children from their neighborhood schools.

The failure of the school board to confront the busing issue puzzled observers from the start and alienated both its more militant supporters and its opponents. To the former the members seemed either cowardly or disingenuous; to the latter they seemed outright liars. In reality, they were in a bind from which they could not extricate themselves. Some of their liberal advisers insisted that they must move slowly; others demanded "Freedom Now." No matter which way they went, they feared they would alienate some. Moreover, if they acknowledged that they planned to bus children for racial balance (which they all still insist they did not), a storm of protest threatened. If, on the other hand, they tried to calm the hysteria by pledging that they would not bus (which they did repeatedly), they were not believed. Realizing that they were in a damned-if-you-do-and-damned-if-you-don't vise, and unable to act out one side or the other of the dilemma, they clung sturdily to the most untenable and unbelievable of all positions — that they believed in integration but did not support busing.

When I asked board members how they could have believed it possible to integrate Richmond's schools without busing, one liberal replied:

> Really, we never considered two-way busing at that time; we knew it was not politically feasible. We felt that the board had an obligation to lead the community, but not to get so far out in front as to lose the district. We were trying, perhaps naïvely, to get people to go along with us, and we believed absolutely what we were saying. Busing to relieve overcrowd-

ing was seen as the vehicle by which people would get used to the idea. But the conservatives sensed better than the liberals where this was going. They insisted on confronting the issue of moving kids for purposes of overcrowding and calling it integration. We really thought we were telling the truth; we believed what we were saying. We thought that instead of busing we might close up the black schools, or we could have followed the de facto segregation committee's recommendation for an educational corridor down the center of the district.

When I answered that the educational corridor was such a long-range plan that even with the funds it would take twenty years to achieve, he said sadly: "I know. I guess we really didn't think we could get far with integration, but we wanted to keep trying."

Another board member suggested also that they had in mind some partial measures that, while falling short of integrating the classrooms, would bring black and white children together in other ways.

I thought we could develop a research center with a good library, maybe laboratories, etc. Youngsters could come together from black and white schools to work together for a couple of weeks. So there were other things we could have done besides getting kids together in the class that would have been useful. These would have provided a bridge to total integration; it would have gotten people used to the idea.

Yet none of these very moderate thoughts was shared with the public. While the reasons for the disparity between their public behavior and private thoughts may be complicated, they are not a product of accidental circumstances. First, members of the board were under conflicting external pressures — blacks demanding integration, and most whites insisting that the status quo be maintained; some of their white liberal advisers cautioning "go slow," and others crying "full speed ahead." Second, they were under two sets of conflicting internal pressures. I have already spoken of one — that ideologically they were committed to both integration and quality education but were fearful of the impact of the former on the latter. The other may have been more important. Politically they were caught between their coexistent beliefs in popular democracy (with all that implies about mass participation) and in leadership by an elite meritocracy— clashing beliefs that call for contradictory actions, and that often immobilize the liberal political actor.

Classical democratic theory rests upon the premise that citizen involvement in political life is essential both to the full development of individual capacites and to the democracy itself. Addressing the dilemma of leadership in a society that honors those principles, Peter Bachrach has written: [3]

> This [does] not preclude guidance and encouragement of elites in the educational process, but, contrary to the premises of elitism, it [does] preclude a relationship of elite domination and creativity, and of non-elite submissiveness and passivity.

But, of course, the line between domination and education is both thin and shifting, and thoughtful men and women have long been concerned about its demarcation.

The crux of the classical theory of democracy lies in an optimistic belief in the growth potential of men, the belief not only that they can and wish to participate, but that it would benefit both the individual and the society if they did so. Ideally, the liberal board members accepted the basic premises, but in reality they were quite pessimistic about the capacity of men, and were frightened of large-scale participation in decision-making.

This distrust of the ordinary citizen as a political participant lies deep within American political ideology. It was one of the central concerns of the Federalists[4] and has remained a core problem for American political theorists and practitioners. In the aftermath of the totalitarian mass movements that shook the world in the 1930s, social scientists turned their attention to a study of fascism.[5] A major outcome of the effort was the development of the notion of the authoritarian personality[6]— the individual who gives rigid adherence to conventional middle-class values, who is submissive and uncritical toward established authority, who identifies with important power figures, and who is closed-minded, ethnocentric and intolerant of those who would violate conventional mores.[7] The merits of that formulation need not detain us; its importance here lies only in the fact that such ideas have been diffused among the liberal, literate sector of the American people, among whom can be counted the liberal leaders in the RUSD.*

Following in that research tradition and spurred on by the rise of McCarthyism, during the 1950s American social scientists sought ways to specify the conditions that would ensure democracy and yet limit participation. Reflecting upon the work of that decade, in 1967 Robert Dahl, a leading pluralist theorist, wrote:

> Perhaps because totalitarian change was so great a danger, political theorists, sociologists, and many other students of democratic life began to place heavier stress on the conditions necessary for a *stable* democracy. Perhaps because internal conflict had grown so menacing, they also focused on *consensus. Thus stability and consensus each became a sort of fetish, particularly among American political and social scientists.* By contrast, conflict and change was perceived not so

---

* The five white, liberal' school board members were: a social scientist at the university; a research scientist and an engineer, both high executives at Standard Oil; and two women, one a widow whose husband had been a government official, the other the wife of a university professor, both of whom had been "civic leaders" long before they came to the school board.

much as offering the possibility of a better future (as democratic ideologues a century earlier would have said), but as
menacing the foundations of existing democracy itself.[8]
[*Emphasis added.*]

Typical of that "fetish" is the assertion by Bernard Berelson and his associates:

> . . . liberal democracy is more than a political system in
> which individual voters and political institutions operate. For
> political democracy to survive, other features are required:
> the intensity of conflict must be limited, the rate of change
> must be restrained, stability in the social and economic struc-
> ture must be maintained, a pluralistic social organization
> must exist, and a basic consensus must bind together the con-
> tending parties. Such features of the system of political
> democracy belong neither to the constitutive institutions nor
> to the individual voter. It might be said that they form the
> atmosphere or the environment in which both operate.[9]

From such efforts developed the theory of democratic
elitism, whose major premise is that democracy can survive
only when power resides in the hands of a group of autono-
mous, competing elites.[10] In this system democracy is said to
be ensured because groups of specialized leaders compete on
behalf of their respective constituencies for their places in
the political sun; because these elites periodically are ac-
countable to an electorate; and because the system is open
at many points for those who would organize to gain access
to elite power.[11] Profoundly suspicious of mass participation,
theorists of democratic elitism argue that leaders must be insulated from mass pressures,[12] and in fact that a healthy
democracy depends upon low levels of participation.[13]

I do not mean to suggest that the liberal leaders read
a handbook of liberal pluralism and democratic elitism and
practiced their political roles accordingly. Rather, there are
two points to be made here. The first is simply that many

of the concepts generated by those theories have been diffused widely enough to have become part of the folk wisdom of the highly educated upper-middle-class liberals who were leaders in the RUSD. Almost every liberal respondent, for example, made some comment suggesting that the conservatives had authoritarian personalities, that they were ideologues, that they were irrational, and that their sudden emergence into the political arena threatened the fundaments of democracy.

The second is that the political system itself exacts a particular kind of behavior, and the liberal leaders in Richmond acted in accordance with the models of political behavior available to them. The study commission and public hearings have long been used to give that system the trappings of democracy and consensus.* Theorists of liberal pluralism have examined these performances, described them in detail, and enshrined the whole system as the exemplar of democracy.[14] For example, in a typical statement that starts from the premise that the conditions for a classical democracy no longer exist in America and that, therefore, the theory has ceased to work, Berelson and his associates conclude:

> And yet, the system that has grown out of classic democratic theory, and, in this country, out of quite different and even elementary social conditions, does continue to work — *perhaps even more vigorously and effectively than ever.*[15] [*Emphasis added.*]

Setting their judgments apart, if we grant that many of the empirical observations of the pluralist theorists are valid, then the question is not really how elites get socialized into

---

* When the conservatives took over the school board and ran the "performances," the liberals hurled charges at them ranging from "undemocratic" to "authoritarian" to "fascist" — charges that are not totally without foundation, but which carry with them a certain irony in view of their own behavior when they were in power.

the existing political system and how they learn political roles and behavior, for, as Berelson says, it is a part of "the atmosphere or the environment in which [they] operate." Rather, it is how a few manage to escape that socialization process.

I am suggesting then that everything in their lives prepared the five men and women who were school board members for their roles as elite leaders — the two women civic leaders, the university professor, the high-level research and business executives. By education, by training, and by their style of life, they were prepared to assume leadership roles in the society. While there were differences among them — some leaned to the right, others to the left; some were more naïve politically, others more astute — they shared a common belief that their status accorded them some special qualities of leadership, and they believed the argument (implicit or explicit) of many leading theorists of democratic elitism that the health of the system depends on the passivity of the great mass of citizens.[16] Commenting on this widespread belief in the American society, Melvin Tumin has written:

> Perhaps most widespread of all today is that rationale which rests the claim of entitlement to superior power upon the supposedly greater wisdom, experience, skill, or knowledge of the powerful. This is a beguiling rationale, for the powerful almost always insist that they use their power in the best interests of the powerless. Under this rubric we find such relationships as that between doctor and patient, parent and child, teacher and pupil, social worker and client, majority group and immigrant group, and rich nation and poor nation. Paternalism in these relationships is usually explicitly acknowledged and, if a "liberal conscience" happens to plague the powerful, the paternalism is sometimes explicitly regretted, but, nevertheless, asserted as unavoidable and required for the best interests of all concerned.[17]

A fitting description of the liberal leadership in Richmond.

But if it is true that the liberal leaders in the RUSD were influenced by the elitism of political practices in America — an elitism that was given legitimacy by liberal social scientists — and if at some level they believed that the foundation of democracy rests on a system of competing elites, then why was there no serious effort to work out some accommodation with the conservative elites? The liberals argue that they did try to persuade and accommodate, but there is no evidence of compromise on any substantive educational issue. And there were certainly no attempts to offer incentives to the working class and lower-middle class that might have allayed their fears and made integration more acceptable. The reason for this failure to negotiate seriously was, I believe, that the liberal leaders did not see the new conservatives as a legitimate elite worthy of competition. Instead, they contemptuously characterized them as an irrational and ideological mass, uninterested in the welfare of the society as a whole, a threat to democratic values, and therefore unfit to participate in the political process.*

Such notions, too, have a long history in Western thought.[18] They are given legitimacy and credibility in the modern era by mass society theorists who present images of an anomic mass readily mobilized by demagogic leaders,[19] and by the students of McCarthyism and other American mass movements who failed to see the phenomena they study as the expressions of real grievances or legitimate interests.[20]

Thus, ambivalent and conflicted, torn between a belief in the merits of popular democracy and a deep suspicion of mass

---

* This fixation on the conservative anti-integrationists as the ultimate evil helped to provide the liberals with an explanation for their failure. The conservatives, they insisted, could be dealt with in the normal processes of political negotiation. Maybe so, but they never really tried.

participation in the political process, the liberal school board members were never able to choose one side or the other of their contradictory political ideology. They neither insulated themselves from mass pressures and led (although the institutional supports for such autonomy did exist), nor did they encourage and permit meaningful participation in decision-making. Instead, they relied on the time-tested tools of liberal politics — the lay study commission and the public hearing — devices that generally are effective as democratic "performances" when the issue is not of immediate concern to any significant sector of the public. *When the issues become important and emotionally charged, however, people are not so readily managed.*

Complicating their dilemma was the American tendency to distrust power — even to deny its existence — which is directly related to the two strains in American political philosophy I have been discussing. Add the myth that schools are nonpolitical and that school men are not political actors which is imbedded in the folklore of school systems[21] and which was deeply felt by all these men and women, and it is no longer difficult to understand why the school board members never seemed to grasp the fact that they had both the power and the legal authority to mandate school integration and busing. In fact, when after his defeat in 1967, Terry Hatter, the only black man ever to serve on the board, offered a motion that the district integrate all grades beginning in September 1967, his four colleagues were so dumbfounded that the motion died for lack of a second, an experience Hatter still remembers with bitterness.[22] When I asked the four white men and women why they had not responded to that motion, they looked bewildered and wondered aloud how they could possibly have done so in the face of the growing opposition. One said very simply, "How could we? Anyhow Terry didn't really mean it," a claim Hatter disputes vigorously. When asked about the incident, he said:

> I felt pretty bad about that, but I had come to expect that sort of thing from those people. I knew I was dealing with people of good heart, but who felt that their mission was to hold things together, not to cause any more conflict. . . . I'm not sure I spoke to anyone for a long while after that May meeting. Their explanations for their failures to support that motion were less than persuasive; always in the interest of keeping the lid on, of keeping things calm. . . . I really couldn't believe it when I didn't even get a second to the motion. . . . Once the issue was up for discussion it seemed possible that we could even swing it. I'm very fond of them all; they're people of good heart; but maybe we just don't need any more nice guys. . . . I always tried to tell them that they had to take a stand, and then those who were with them would stand firm, and those against would be so anyway. Instead, they did nothing and got everybody mad at them. Now they're terribly hurt.

In sum, all together these strains and the cross-pressures they exerted effectively immobilized this liberal board. To act out one side of any of the dilemmas that bound them was to abandon the principles that upheld the other side. So, they vacillated both publicly and privately. It was not a simple matter of being disingenuous as some liberals charged, nor of being outright liars as some conservatives charged. They were human actors caught between what were for them competing and equally valid claims. In such situations men hesitate, they hedge, they falter, and they often fail.

CHAPTER 6 **THE ELECTORATE STIRS: 1967**

The stage was set for a test of strength between the factions when, in April 1967, the terms of two board members, Walter Fauerso and Terry Hatter, were to expire.

CCNS, the neighborhood schools organization, was a small group that never attempted to develop a wide membership base in the community. Its decisions were made by a small core of leaders who assumed that their position on the politically sensitive issue of busing and integration would rally people to their support. While it had its roots in the burgeoning right wing of the district, CCNS remained careful about complicity with the John Birch Society. Several people reported that when one of the early members made his Birch affiliation known, he was asked to resign his office. Eager to make me understand how separate from the Birch Society CCNS was, one organizer proudly announced,

"The Birch Society has a dossier on me, and I'm known among the Birchers as a 'comsymp.'"

As the election approached, however, they knew they could not make a respectable showing without substantial help. Therefore, they gathered together a coalition of individuals, groups, and organizations representing the right wing of the political spectrum to participate in the selection of candidates. Before the end of 1966 one candidate, Goy Fuller, who had been active in the neighborhood schools movement from the beginning, had agreed to run. The choice of the second candidate was more problematic, as the broad coalition of the right led to ideological struggles that made consensus difficult. "We had arguments and splits within the group about candidates," said one informant. "There were internal problems that we had to resolve." The major "problem" was establishing ideological purity, with those further to the right insisting that they would accept no deviation. In addition, most people who might have been acceptable were hesitant to get mixed up in what held the prospect of being a messy fight, especially when victory seemed so remote.

It was not until about the end of February, just six weeks before the election, that a second candidate, Virgil Gay, was selected. But within a week some of the groups participating in the selection began to fall out over him. Indeed, there was so much opposition to his candidacy that CCNS, fearful that the whole movement would become immobilized over the issue, decided unilaterally to support only Fuller. But the potential political managers and financial angels of the campaign insisted upon a unified slate as the price of their participation, and cooler heads prevailed. CCNS stayed with the slate.

Getting the campaign off the ground was not easy, first because they were political novices, second because they were opposed by Richmond's "respectable" establishment, and third because none of the leaders really thought they could win. For example, candidate Goy Fuller said,

> I suppose I thought there was some remote chance of winning. My wife didn't think we'd win. And Virgil Gay wasn't even here during the last week of the campaign, not even on election night. We called him up to tell him the results. But we needed a forum for our point of view and the election campaign could serve that. I guess the real purpose of the whole thing was to force a promise from the board that they would keep the neighborhood schools intact.

Virgil Gay commented,

> Both my wife and I thought we'd lose because we were opposed by the *Richmond Independent* [the only daily newspaper in the district], Standard Oil, and everybody.

And, indeed, the *Independent* enthusiastically endorsed Fauerso and Hatter, and Standard Oil encouraged Fauerso (one of their top executives) to run and contributed to both his and Hatter's campaigns. Even the very conservative Richmond Council of Industries failed to support the challengers.

While I have no evidence on the matter, it is interesting to speculate about the reasons for the position of the business community. First, in general, it is in their interest to maintain stable community relations and to keep social discord at a minimum. For one thing, a community in conflict is not likely to facilitate the recruitment and retention of an executive staff. For another, when a conflict escalates, there is no way to know who will get caught in the fallout. Second, although conservatives, these members of the establishment were moderates who were wary of the new and noisy breed growing up on the political right. They did not like their manners, their mores, or their ideological rigidity. Temperamentally and socially the leaders of Richmond's business community were closer to the upper-middle-class liberals than to the lower-middle-class conservatives who dominated CCNS. Third, the business elite had by then developed a coalition with the liberals that worked quite satisfactorily for them, since on those issues that were central to their interests, they retained final control. For example, I am told that no major school matter, such as a request for a tax increase, went before the public without their approval.

In addition to their inability to garner support from any significant part of the business community, the conservatives were hindered by their inexperience in politics. Few in CCNS had ever been involved in a political campaign before; fewer still had any idea of how to organize one. One sympathetic and experienced political observer reported,

> Six weeks before the 1967 election there was still no precinct organization, everyone was fighting everyone else, and there was no money. [The campaign] got off the ground no more than one month before election day.

Troubled as the conservatives were, the liberals were even more so. With CCNS the conservatives at least had the nucleus of an organization; the liberals had none. While the conservatives had ideological differences, their fear of integration was strong enough to enable them to set those differences aside; not so with the liberals whose ideological rifts were carried with them right into the campaign when, deciding that the incumbent board could not be trusted to proceed forthrightly with an integration plan, the left liberal faction fielded a third candidate who campaigned for INTEGRATION NOW.

Adding to the liberal woes, and giving the faltering conservative campaign a powerful boost, the school board, prodded by its superintendent, released the CACDFS report six weeks before the election. By then the committee had been in existence for eighteen months. For the several months immediately before the release of the report, it had been working outside the glare of the public spotlight, and public anxiety about it had abated. Why, then, was the report released at such an awkward political moment? Those who were responsible looked at me vacantly when I asked that question; they did not seem to know how to answer. One said, "It was ready." Another, "It came out, and there was nothing else to do." While there seems to be no satisfactory answer (although some embittered critics attribute it to "the liberal death wish"), I suspect that the act was born of the stubborn hope that the growing conflict was still amenable to discussion and persuasion. If people read the report, the liberal members probably reasoned, they would see that their worst fears were groundless. At the same time they probably still had some idea that the "official" pronouncements of an "officially constituted" public body would legitimate the cause of integration. Yet, irrationally enough, they did nothing to publicize the report's rather mild recommendations in the time between its release and the election. It was weeks *after* the election before any of those recommendations were put on the school board agenda for public discussion, and then only the minor ones. In fact, they never did get around to discussing the report's major recommendation for the reorganization of the district schools into a 4-4-4 grade plan, whereby Grades 1 through 4 would provide elementary education, Grades 5 through 8 would provide intermediate education, and Grades 9 through 12 would provide high school education. They just let it die.

Those speculations aside, all members of that board now agree that the timing was devastating politically. There probably would be no quarrel among them with this statement from one of their colleagues.

The timing turned out to be terrible on the De Facto Segregation Report. The report originally had been scheduled to be given to us early in the year, but the committee wasn't

> quite ready. They hadn't done all they wanted to do yet, and we didn't want to rush them too much. When the report was finally ready to be submitted, it came one month before the election. It scared people to death. They thought that we were going the same route as Berkeley.

Notice the language of those comments. The timing "turned out" to be terrible; the report "came" one month before the election. It is as if the report had a will of its own, as if there had been no human agency. Yet the report could not have "come out" if the board had not invited it, or, at the very least, permitted it.

Practical political advisers urged that it be held up until July 1 when school would have been out and public attention diverted from school affairs to vacation plans, but their pleas went unheeded. One informant said, "Many of us pleaded with them to hold it up. We argued that the opposition would pull phrases out of context, that it would be tossed in as a campaign issue, that it would be completely distorted." And that is exactly what happened. The report was picked up by the conservative campaigners and brandished like a cudgel. They moved back and forth across the district, waving the report before their listeners' eyes and repeating, "This says they're going to put your children on buses and send them all over this district."

In truth, the report said nothing of the kind. So concerned were the members of CACDFS about the growing crisis over elementary school education, that they recommended that elementary schools (which in the reorganization plan they suggested would have served grades 1 through 4) should retain the neighborhood school concept, a compromise they thought would be acceptable both to the community and to the board whose depth of commitment to integration was unclear even to them. With reference to busing, the report said merely that it was a well established practice in American public school education; that it had been used extensively in the Richmond schools; that the district was at that time (1965/1966) busing 2,320 elementary school children, all in the north end; and that "the community's suspicion of and hostility to busing is to a large extent the result of the district's own ambiguous and contradictory policy."[1]

Unfortunately, few people ever read the well reasoned, mildly written report, with its relatively moderate recommendations. The conservative challengers hammered away at the charge that the board was planning "forced two-way busing," and it was difficult to hear the reasonable replies of the board members.

As the campaign proceeded and the conservative scare tactics escalated, the liberal incumbents became more frightened and more defensive. At no time did they take a firm stand on integration. In the ballot arguments that went to every voter in the district *neither Fauerso nor Hatter mentioned integration or busing.* When their challengers demanded that they publicly and unequivocally state their positions on busing, they refused, saying that their commitment was to "quality education." Talking about the campaign, one incumbent reported:

> The question most frequently asked was: Are you for or against neighborhood schools? I refused to answer that question. The neighborhood school is only a mirror of the neighborhood. So to be for or against neighborhood schools is not to speak to the issue. The issue is finding a way to help youngsters learn. We wanted to talk about quality education; all they wanted to talk about was busing.

Finally, on the weekend immediately preceding the election, they placed a large advertisement in the local newspapers:

> Incumbent school board members Fauerso and Hatter have not endorsed mass busing of children as falsely claimed by their opponents.

In response to such statements, their opponents charged hypocrisy. One neighborhood schools candidate said,

> They were just hypocrites. Everyone knew they were for busing but they didn't have the nerve to stand up and fight for what they believed in. They always weaseled out of answering the questions and tried to insist they were talking about education. But what's racial balance got to do with education?

Meanwhile, the neighborhood schools candidates were conjuring up images of small children shivering pitifully in the rain as they waited for buses, of wrecked buses and mangled bodies, of frightened children wandering in the darkness, left behind at school by a heartless and unthinking bus driver. Many of those most fearful and angry, remember, were the parents of the same children who were already being bused to school without drama or fanfare.

These were the fears that were publicly expressed. There were others that were talked about in whispers which may have been the more powerful — fears for the children's safety, both physically and sexually, which at least in part sounded like projections of their own suppressed emotions. Several respondents said, for example, that they were afraid their children would be beaten up. "You know, they're violent people," said one man who had just finished telling me that he would "kill anyone who thinks he can put my kids on a bus and send them down there." Another said, "They hate us whites. I'm not going to let my kids go where they're hated, and I don't see why they'd want their kids to either." Two others said that they could conceive of sending boys to school in the ghetto, but never girls. "What's the difference?" I asked. "Those colored boys just can't be trusted. You know how they are," was one response. Another suggested, "You just go over to Berkeley and find out what goes on there. They don't like to talk about it over there, but everyone knows that little girls have been molested."

In sum, with a public that was becoming ever more anxious, the incumbents refused to discuss the question that was on everyone's mind. When at the last minute they issued a weak statement that they had not endorsed mass busing but offered no alternative integration program, they were unconvincing. As one of their opponents said,

> Who could believe them? Most people wrote it off — and rightly so — as a cheap election trick. After all, they'd been sitting on the board all the time we were pleading with them to promise not to bus our children, and they ignored us along with the rest.

Thus, the incumbents lost whatever opportunity they might have had to educate the public, and they deprived their campaign of the positive thrust that might have helped to confront and expose the bigotry of the adherents of neighborhood schools.*

The final blow came to the liberal cause when, two weeks before the election, the superintendent announced that he intended to hold a conference in Santa Rosa (a community fifty miles from Richmond) on the weekend immediately preceding the election to discuss the CACDFS report. Several of his supporters and staff members reported that they gasped in disbelief and pleaded with him to change his mind. The report was causing enough trouble, they argued; why focus on it any more? Furthermore, it would take people away from the campaign on the very weekend when they should be manning the telephones and walking the precincts. But their arguments went unheeded, and the weekend conference took place as scheduled, removing from the district just three days before the election all the adminis-

---

* Cf. Reginald G. Damerell, *Triumph in a White Suburb*, where it is argued that in Teaneck, New Jersey, the firm stand on integration taken by the liberals exposed the racist nature of the opposition and paved the way for a liberal victory.

trators, many of the teachers, and substantial numbers of lay people who supported integration. Meanwhile, the conservatives were ringing doorbells with the de facto committee report in one hand and news of the conference in the other.

The figures in Table 10 show that the three liberal candidates combined garnered 1,464 votes more than the conservatives, with Phillips, the left liberal candidate who had taken a strong pro-integration stand polling 5,230 votes. From this distance, it is extremely difficult to assess the meaning of that Phillips vote. Many of the liberal leaders insist that Phillips was the "spoiler," that if he had not been in the race, Fauerso and Hatter would have won. They argue that, since it was very unlikely that any significant number of the Phillips votes would have gone to the conservatives, those 5,230 votes distributed between the incumbents would have assured a victory. But that ignores two possibilities: first, that many Phillips voters might have just stayed home if he had not offered an alternative to the incumbents; second, that many of the Phillips votes were what in election politics are called "single-shot" — a vote for only one of the two open seats.

There is no way to assess the first possibility, but a review of the precinct count in that election indicates that both

Table 10. Results of the RUSD School Board
Election, April 18, 1967[a]

Candidate	Liberal	Conservative
Walter Fauerso	9,275	
Terry Hatter	9,958	
Paul Phillips	5,230	
Goy Fuller		11,610
Virgil Gay		11,389
TOTAL	24,463	22,999

SOURCE: Contra Costa County Registration-Election Department.
[a] Registration was 68,993; 25,378 (36.8 percent) people voted.

Phillips and Hatter supporters often single-shot their votes. For example, in four white precincts where Phillips was strong, Fauerso polled 756 votes, Hatter 812, and Phillips 348. There is a 56 vote difference between Fauerso and Hatter. Assuming that all 56 votes went to Phillips, that still leaves 292 Phillips votes which, we can reasonably infer, were single-shot votes. Similarly, in the black community where Hatter, a black man, ran very strongly and Fauerso very weakly, the pattern of single-shotting votes for Hatter was evident. In five black precincts examined, Fauerso drew 441 votes, Hatter 1,451, and Phillips 663. The difference between Fauerso and Hatter here was 1,010, of which 663 went to Phillips. That leaves 347 votes which were probably single-shots for Hatter.

Others, including Fauerso, argue that at least he could have retained his seat if Phillips had not been in the race. The Phillips campaign, they say, drew from Fauerso the white, left liberal voters, most of whom would also have cast ballots for Hatter. Thus, they reason, Phillips drew little from Hatter, and the latter's total of 9,958 probably represented close to his total vote getting ability. But again, that argument is predicated on the assumption that those who voted for Phillips — black and white — would have voted for Fauerso instead, and it fails to consider the strong Phillips vote in the black community and the single-shot voting patterns.

Whatever the validity of these speculations, there are some things we do know. The incumbents came into the election unable or unwilling to take a firm position on integration and busing at a time when community passions on both sides were mounting. They faced the electorate with their own constituency divided — three candidates running for two seats — and handicapped by the release of the CACDFS report six weeks earlier and by a conference on the weekend before election day that took many of their active supporters out of the district for discussion of that report. The conservatives may have been right when they estimated early in the campaign that they probably could not win. How could they know that the ineptitude of the liberals and their inability to set aside their differences would hand them an election victory? In retrospect, what is puzzling is not that the liberals lost, but that they so narrowly missed.

With the seating of the two neighborhood schools representatives on the school board July 1, 1967, the conflict took on new depth. The Fuller-Gay victory publicly legitimated the anti-integration position, and many people who had hesitated to associate with those who had been labeled rabble-rousers now felt freed to act out their fears and prejudices.

Fuller and Gay never let up on the busing issue. They held the threat aloft for public attention and scrutiny, making certain that public fears did not abate. Indeed, Fuller viewed that task as his central mission:

> I viewed my own position in two ways, the most important one was to alert the people to what the board had in store for them. . . . I was very successful in that item.

The split board reflected the split community; each meeting was like the coming together of two warring factions. Reasonable discourse soon came to an end. Instead, each side shouted slogans and epithets at the other; most discussions were peppered with hooting, jeering, and applauding by partisans in the audience. On any but the most trivial issue the board could be counted on to split 3-2; seemingly routine matters quickly became transformed into arguments about busing. Discussions of educational policy and financing were pushed into the background, as in meeting after meeting there were disputes about using Elementary and Secondary Education Act (ESEA) Title 1 funds to bus children from overcrowded ghetto schools to empty classrooms elsewhere in the district, about setting new attendance area boundaries, about in-service training programs in intergroup relations, and more.

Every suggestion to relieve overcrowding in ghetto schools was construed by Fuller and Gay to be a precedent-setting plot — a foot in the door that would ultimately legitimate large-scale two-way busing — and was fought strenuously. In fact, they were not completely wrong, for while the majority members publicly insisted that these transfers were only to relieve overcrowding, privately they admitted that this was their way of accustoming the community to the sight of black faces in their schools. "With time," one board member said, "we thought people would get used to the idea." Sometimes that strategy works, but in this case it was more like pulling an adhesive bandage from a wound slowly. It just hurt all the more; and with each pain the conservative political base expanded. Anti-busing groups sprang up all over the district, and their attendance at board meetings swelled.

At the same time, the divided board reflected and highlighted community divisions in educational philosophy and in matters pertaining to school financing, differences that helped to further polarize the already divided community. Where before the approval of expenditures was routine, now they were questioned closely, and the conservatives accused the administration of profligate spending. Where earlier, the approval of courses and textbooks had been perfunctory, now it became the subject of intense debate. Where two years before, the proposals of the Parents for Educational Decency had received less than serious attention from the board, now those people and others like them had two spokesmen on the board who carried the fight for them.

While board meetings grew more heated, both liberals and conservatives were moving to strengthen and consolidate their positions. The conservatives, sensing that they had the political advantage as large numbers of Middle Americans began to respond angrily to the convulsive social movements of the sixties, turned their major efforts toward the political arena. The liberals, fearful that they would be engulfed by this awakening, hedged their political bets with an appeal to the courts.

THE POLITICAL CONTEXT OF POLARIZATION

In a city where school system and city boundaries are coterminous, the residents have ties to political, social, and service institutions that may provide a common framework, as well as the ground rules, for the resolution of an incipient conflict. Within the framework of the city, interest groups will tend to compromise, accommodate, and trade to keep the conflict within acceptable bounds. Thus, while a large city may have as diverse and heterogeneous a population as the RUSD, it is bound together by more than a school system. People in a city must live and work together in many arenas of social and political life, and they develop some experience in uniting for action in a common cause — a transit system, a protest over inadequate garbage collection, construction that violates aesthetic sensibilities.

But the RUSD is an aggregate of relatively independent communities with no such common core or common cause. The district sprawls over 110 square miles and encompasses five cities and several unincorporated territories. Each city has its own political organizations and institutions for public welfare and safety; each unincorporated area supplies some services to its residents and relies on neighboring cities or the county for the rest. Consequently, instead of providing the potential for mediating the conflict, local political institutions were quite readily mobilized to take sides in the struggle. The city councils of the several cities all found themselves pressured to take public positions on the issues in contest; some even appeared at school board meetings to apprise the board formally and publicly of their stands.

While the city councils have no formal power with reference to school board policy, the informal pressures can be very great. For the cities, eager to recruit business and industry to expand their tax bases, the school system is a selling point. A controversial integration plan and a community torn apart over school strife is hard to sell. Thus, the school district is under pressure to keep things cool, since, if the cities do enlarge their tax bases successfully, the district shares in the increased revenue. Moreover, in the daily course of organizational life, the school system and the cities often trade favors and services, and harmonious relations facilitate such negotiations.

From the standpoint of those who opposed the school board's integration policy, there was also great psychological value in involving their local governments. First, at the very time when these opposition forces were meeting with little success in affecting the formulation of school district policy, they were able to influence the political process in their home communities quite successfully. For example, the councils of El Cerrito, San Pablo, Pinole, and Hercules all opposed the busing plan. Richmond's city council failed to take a formal stand on the issue; its two black councilmen served to neutralize that body. Informally, however, the white councilmen articulated their opposition. And each such victory lent the conservative cause an aura of rightness and righteousness to which they could point and from which they could take heart. Almost all of the conservative respondents enumerated for me triumphantly the local city agencies that were on their side.

Second, it enabled them to keep their troops busy, always useful in a political struggle. Hundreds of people had been mobilized and were eager to do something for the cause. The conservative leadership kept them working and feeling productive, and one of the ways they accomplished that was by sending delegations to meetings of local agencies and political bodies to keep the pressure on.

THE RECALL CAMPAIGN

After the 1967 election, the lame duck board continued to equivocate on the question of a district-wide integration plan and instead fiddled around with relatively insignificant boundary changes. Their indecisiveness made the conservatives even more edgy than before, and by the time Fuller and Gay were seated in July, the tension in the district had reached new heights.

Through the summer and early fall, the two conservatives kept pushing their three liberal colleagues to take a firm stand against busing, but to no avail. Then, in October 1967 the majority voted to cooperate with the Richmond Redevelopment Agency in building a new school in the redevelopment area, a move that required the district to present a plan for integrating *all* schools in the redevelopment area, in return for which the Redevelopment Agency would advance the construction funds for the new school.

Frustrated, angry, and anxious, the conservatives de-

cided that the time had come to force a showdown. One of
their top political strategists said:

> We estimated that, given the configuration of the school year,
> a major reorganization plan would only be adopted in the
> spring to be implemented in the fall. We figured the liberals
> had two more chances to order integration — in the spring
> of 1968 and 1969. But we weren't really worried about 1969;
> by then we knew we could win the election when those three
> seats would come up. So we knew we had to stop them in
> 1968.

Thus, the strategy was clear: demand that the liberal majority take a firm no-busing position or threaten a recall
movement. Accordingly, at the board meeting of January 31, 1968, Fuller introduced a motion that read:

> The action taken on October 18 giving permission to the ad-
> ministration to develop plans for an integrated school in the
> Crescent Park area and that the district as a whole, shall not
> include developing any plan to establish a racially balanced
> school in the Crescent Park area, or any other school or
> schools in the district, that includes forcible busing of stu-
> dents, or unusual boundary changes, thus preventing students
> from attending their neighborhood school.

The liberal president of the school board presented a
substitute motion that said, in part:

> The board realizes that few parents wish their children to be
> transported from their nearest school, and that it has no in-
> tention of instituting a two-way busing program. For this
> reason the board reaffirms its present busing practices.

Notice the ambiguity of the majority position. In October they had instructed the superintendent to "make recommendations to the board in regard to the Redevelopment
Area which will include some [integration] planning for the
district as a whole"— planning that necessarily meant some

two-way busing, since the only way integrated schools could exist in the redevelopment area was if white children were brought in from outside the neighborhood. Yet three months later they were again insisting that they had "no intention of instituting a two-way busing plan."

After an acrimonious debate, the substitute motion was adopted 3–2, and the stage was set for a movement to recall the most outspoken liberal board member, Maurice Barusch. An organization, Save Our Schools (sos), was formed specially to direct the recall operation, and a petition for recall was filed a few weeks later.

While the movement failed to accomplish its manifest purpose, it did serve to frighten the board majority and to splinter the pro-integration forces in the district.*At the first sign of the recall petition, the more moderate among the liberals responded in panic. Their first thought was to protect Barusch; integration, they said, was dead, at least for the moment. The more militant advocates of integration were outraged. "I'll never be a party to anything that says integration is dead," said one angry liberal leader. Within weeks some of the most integration-minded blacks and whites in the district formed the Legal Action Committee for Equal Schools (laces), a biracial, middle-class organization that took the position that integration in the rusd would only be achieved in the courts. The court action that this group stimulated a few months later was to play a central role in the dramatic climax of this story.

Meanwhile, not only had the conservatives successfully paralyzed the board majority and splintered the liberals, they once again broadened and deepened their base in the community. They went into the recall campaign relatively naïve about their own constituency.

---

* They gathered only 13,000 of the 17,000 signatures necessary to place the matter before the voters.

> I was dumbfounded about how little the public knew about all that was going on; how little public concern there was. It took sitting down and talking with people for five, ten, or fifteen minutes to make them understand what was happening and that the board was really on the verge of busing their children.

They came out with 13,000 signatures.

> While it wasn't successful, we did get 13,000 signatures and we did keep the board off balance. More important, we now had in our hands 13,000 names, addresses, and phone numbers of people who were on our side and could be counted on during the next election.

Recall that the 1967 election had been won with just a little more than 11,000 votes, and the political potential of those 13,000 signators becomes apparent.*

THE COURT ACTION

At about the time LACES was born, the Contra Costa Legal Services Foundation (CCLSF), a federally funded agency that had been operating in Richmond for about six months, began to investigate the possibility of bringing a desegregation suit against the RUSD.[1] While the district is large, news travels fast, and it was only a matter of time before LACES and CCLSF got together; within a few months LACES had given the Foundation its unequivocal support.

After much deliberation on the merits of a district-wide suit *versus* a suit involving only one school, the latter strategy was adopted. On October 16, 1968, suit was filed against the RUSD in the Contra Costa Superior Court involving the almost all black Verde Elementary School and the three predominantly white schools in the adjoining neighborhood.[2] The Verde Suit, as it soon came to be known,

* At the time there were 68,993 voters in the district.

alleged that the student population of the school was more than 99 percent black, that no white students were in attendance there, that white students living in the Verde attendance area were permitted to attend other elementary schools, that three adjacent schools either had no black students or a negligible percentage, that the Verde school had been constructed in 1951 to create racial segregation in previously integrated public schools adjoining Verde, and that its mandatory attendance boundaries were drawn and maintained to promote and preserve this racial segregation.

The action asked the court to prohibit the use of additional facilities then under construction at Verde "except to implement the elimination of racial imbalance." Accompanying the suit were three alternative plans for desegregating Verde, all involving some two-way busing of students between Verde, Dover, Broadway, and Lake schools. With the filing of the suit, the conflict escalated again, and the polarization of the community was almost complete; communication ceased.*

The board met one week after the suit was filed, ostensibly to decide whether to contest it. As with the public meetings of the Committee on De Facto Segregation earlier, these public discussions were a sham, little more than a performance through which the liberal majority still hoped to alleviate some of the discontent. For while the majority of the board members had been disturbed and angered about the suit, feeling that their friends had "pulled the rug out from under us," they had known about it in advance and for weeks had been weighing the advice of their divided liberal advisers. The group that had been responsible for instituting the suit exerted great pressure on them not to contest.

---

* It was at about this time that the news media began to show increasing interest in the events in Richmond. In the months that followed, television and newspaper coverage was extensive throughout the Bay Area.

Another faction argued strongly that they should fight and force the court to order integration, the strategy being, as one of them said, "Then they would have something solid to stand on." By the time the suit came under public discussion, the three liberal board members already knew that they would not contest it; the decision that confronted them was how best not to do so.* One of the board majority told me,

> Originally when the suit was planned we had not thought of not contesting. It was after many [private] discussions with others that we finally came to the decision that we couldn't contest the suit. As we listened to the arguments, it seemed that there was no way to deny the allegations.

Another said,

> Once it [the suit] was a fact, we didn't see much to argue with in the basic facts which were the basis for that suit. Everything they said about Verde School was true.

Even the *Richmond Independent* editorialized on November 11, 1968, in favor of not contesting the suit.

> It is highly improbable that the school board could win if it fought this action. As presently constituted the operations at Verde are in violation of the Civil Rights bill and the Supreme Court ruling on integration . . . . It seems to us that Dr. Widel's program or a reasonable alternative should be approved. . . . [The] Verde School proposal should have the full support of the voters and the people.

Meanwhile, once it became public, the conservative community exerted enormous pressure to contest the suit. Thousands of people — supporters and opponents of integration — attended that first discussion meeting, but it

---

* With the decision not to contest the suit, a victory went to the plaintiffs by default.

was the conservative anger that dominated the room. The atmosphere was explosive, and, as usual when tempers were high, the conservatives had a more difficult time than ordinarily in concealing their racial hostilities. One man, a leader of the major anti-integration organization in the district, demanded to know why the majority board members "feel that they *owe* integration even when it is against the best interests of the majority." Another insisted, "Caucasians have rights also. Why is everyone always concerned about *them* instead of us?"

On a 3–2 vote the majority decided to ask for a thirty-day continuance to allow time for the development of integration plans. Again, their failure to act decisively only heightened tempers and anxieties that were already too high.

At another public session two weeks later the superintendent submitted to the board a plan for the integration of Verde with Broadway and Dover schools (which soon became known as the B-V-D plan) that called for converting Verde and Broadway into schools serving kindergarten through Grade 3, while Dover would handle Grade 4 through 6.* Of course, the plan required transporting children from their neighborhood schools. Again, the anti-integrationists, who dominated the audience, exploded in rage.

Still unable to act, the board majority asked the superintendent to present them with some further alternatives. Two weeks later three new plans were submitted for public discussion. Now the district had before it six plans, three that had been submitted with the lawsuit, and three more which were variations on the same theme. Meanwhile, all the racial fears that plague the American psyche had for weeks been rushing to the surface. The ugly phrases "damned niggers" and "nigger-lovin' bastards" were heard around the

---

* Eventually, the plan was modified so that all kindergartners would remain in their neighborhood schools.

meeting room. One woman shouted, "Next they'll be demanding that we invite them to Sunday dinner." Another parent, speaking for the Dover PTA, insisted that "Dover parents will not permit their children to go into an area where adults cannot go by themselves."

The last was a reference to the fact that for people who live in the north end of the district and work at Standard Oil in Richmond, the shortest route to work was through the North Richmond ghetto. After an outburst of black anger in 1966, the company newspaper had advised its employees that for safety's sake they should take an alternate route to work.

Finally, in a last-ditch attempt to sidestep making the necessary decision on busing, the majority voted to ask the court to select among the six plans which one "best meets the requirements of the law." The court promptly threw the ball back to the school board. The problem of selecting an integration plan, it ruled, was a legislative determination; it was not the court's business to legislate.

When I asked the majority members why they had chosen that course, all three said that they believed it would have been easier for the people in the district to accept a plan that had been mandated by the court. Since the legitimacy of such court rulings had already been challenged throughout the land, since the anti-integrationists in the RUSD had already said clearly that no matter how the court ruled, they would not accept it as law, and since the conservative opposition was extremely well organized to carry on the fight, it is hard to understand how they could have so deluded themselves. But they were desperate to cloak their position in legitimacy, and in the face of the conflict that confronted them, they could not draw that sense of legitimacy from what they believed to be the "law of the land." Only positive, or at least accepting, feedback from the conservative anti-integrationists could give them that.

And they had not yet learned that it would never come from that source.

Meanwhile, many advisers of the liberal board members were insisting that to correct the Verde imbalance alone was not consonant with the board's integration policy. The six other schools that were almost completely black also deserved attention, they argued. The three liberals reluctantly agreed, and they asked the superintendent to present plans at the next public meeting for integrating all elementary schools in the district. Thus, on December 18, 1968, after a vituperative debate, the board finally adopted a three-phase integration plan for the entire district — Phase 1 to start in September 1969 and to include the integration of Verde-Broadway-Dover, and Phases 2 and 3 to become effective in September 1970 and 1971, respectively.[3] Livid with anger and frustration, Fuller reminded them that just a year before Mrs. Berry had promised that Richmond would "not go the way of Berkeley," that Dr. Barusch had said that "to bus children ten miles to integrate the schools is not believed by the board to be practical," and that all three had assured the people just ten months before that they had "no intention of instituting a two-way busing program."

The entire plan was flawed — conceived in haste by an inept administration — and even the most ardent supporters of integration reported that they had difficulty in accepting it. But perhaps the most paradoxical aspect of the plan was that the first major integration efforts were scheduled to begin in the area of highest resistance, at the Broadway and Dover schools in the heart of San Pablo. The board majority contended that problems of distance, convenience, and the immediate need to correct the Verde imbalance demanded such planning. All that may be true, but there was no reason why the integration of the Kensington and Madera schools, which serve Kensington and the El Cerrito hills, the area that was expected to be least recalcitrant, should not have begun at the same time. Instead, those schools were not scheduled to be integrated until Phase 3 in 1971 — a situation that further enraged the San Pablo people immediately affected, since the hills area had provided the white integrationist leadership and had been the center of the integration drive. Now the people who had so steadfastly opposed busing viewed with considerable bitterness the fact that their children were about to be bused, while the children of those who had worked to impose that situation on them remained securely in their neighborhood schools.

It was not until two weeks before the election of April 1969 that the board majority finally responded to these criticisms by including Kensington and Madera in the first phase of the integration plan. But by then it was too late to undo the damage in the north end of the district, and the move probably served only to bring to the surface the fears that had been relatively dormant in Kensington.

UNITED SCHOOL PARENTS

The organization of the conservatives was aided and stimulated by the tumult and shouting of the months immediately preceding the adoption of the district-wide integration plan. Groups of parents sprang up at once in those white schools named in the suit. They came to the first board meeting at which the suit was discussed and, as one respondent reported, "met parents with similar concerns there and all decided to get together to deal with our problems." Out of these smaller groups and the meetings they held grew the United School Parents (USP), an umbrella organization that quickly coalesced all the anti-integration groups in the district. CCNS and the several smaller parents' organizations disappeared under its aegis, and it soon became a powerful and effective political force — well organized, determined, and tough.

Organizationally, USP was interesting in that it sought to develop units in each of the district's schools, sometimes taking over the existing PTA, sometimes paralleling it. Ultimately, it claimed units in thirty-four of the forty-eight elementary schools and in one of the seven junior-high schools.*

The board of directors of the organization was composed of two members from each unit who elected from among themselves the usual five or so officers that are traditional in such organizations. Thus, at its peak, the board of directors had seventy members, which gave the group immediate access to an unusually large active core so that extraorganization tasks could be attended to quickly and intraorganization communication with the membership could be expedited.

Unlike CCNS which was an elite group, USP was conceived as a mass organization that welcomed anyone who was sympathetic to the cause, and it openly recruited among the right wing elements of the district. Although USP informants disclaimed any Birch Society ties, I had the sense that this was a matter of political tactics rather than ideological differences — a belief that was given some confirmation by one officer of the organization, who said,

> I don't think there are Birch members in USP. But at the last meeting there was a lot of talk about Schmidt [an avowed Bircher] going to the [state] senate, and there was some joking about it and people were quite excited about a Bircher

* No one could or would tell me what the total USP membership was at its peak, although people generally guessed that it ran into many thousands — some thought as high as 10,000. One founder claimed that there were no membership requirements such as dues through which they could keep track. If a person came to a unit meeting and showed interest, he was welcomed. If he wanted to make a contribution, it was gratefully accepted; if not, that was all right, too.

beating out a conservative. They kind of got a kick out of that, and they didn't seem at all worried about the Birch Society.

The mass nature of USP pushed most of the middle-class CCNS leaders into the background. The elected leaders of USP were (and remain) almost exclusively working-class whites from the San Pablo area, which discomfited many middle-class participants. Although the heat of the busing issue encouraged an alliance between the working class and middle class, for many members of the latter it was a union that chafed.* The overt racism that was articulate and rampant often offended middle-class sensibilities, and many left the organization.† Many others who stayed were always a little apologetic. One such respondent explained,

> Some of our people here left because they became convinced the organization was made up of racists. Some people were; they didn't like colored people and didn't care who knew it. I felt a little uncomfortable about that, too, when they would say terrible things.

The differences in educational concerns also distressed middle-class participants. Said one,

* During the election campaign that followed, USP even managed to get a few middle- and upper-middle-class people in Kensington to form a unit. But while that unit participated in the campaign, it was not without a great deal of discomfort over its alliance with "those red-neck types," and as soon as the election was won the unit disbanded. Cf. John Finley Scott and Louis Heyman Scott, "They Are Not So Much Anti-Negro as Pro-Middle Class," which argues that the resistance of the white middle class to integration is due largely to anxieties about status and the concomitant concern for quality education which, in their view, means a white-middle-class school.

† An observer at one early USP organizing meeting reported that "a man who vowed he would 'put on a white robe and take a gun in [my] hand before they'll bus my kids to Richmond' received the loudest and longest applause of the night" (Mark Peppard, "School Desegregation: A Case Study of Polarization Within a Community").

Education is my first concern, and I question the interest in education of a lot of those people . . . There are a lot of people who have strong feelings about a lot of things with little knowledge or understanding. Some of them . . . well, I just don't know how to say it. I question their motives. Some people seem to just need to cause trouble and problems. At the peak we had a conglomeration of people and all got along very well. We all had the same goals. It was very exciting to watch. There were professional people and truck drivers. But as things died down, only certain people remain in. I would say that now it's mostly the working-class people from San Pablo.

It seems likely, therefore, that for most USP members, it was a single issue organization.* Once the busing issue was won, most middle-class participants left, wanting nothing further to do with what some of them called "those Okies." And as with all political organizations, once the battle was over, no amount of effort by the leadership could keep the general membership (or even some of the leaders) from a quick retreat into family and private concerns. One former activist said to me,

I was just glad to have it over with and be able to get back to my private life and the things that really matter. I'm not the joining type, and I don't enjoy running to meetings and all that. I did what I had to do; that's all.

Those sentiments were expressed more than once by others who had played important roles in the initial mobilization.

* The results of the November 1970 election for state assembly-man in the district lend credibility to this speculation. The Republican nominee Goy Fuller, president of the school board, was heavily supported by USP in his attempt to unseat the Democratic incumbent, John Knox. Fuller pitched his campaign around Knox's equivocation on the busing issue. But the issue apparently had little relevance in another political context, for the voters reelected Knox handily, by more than 2-1. Fuller did not carry a single community in the school

CITIZENS FOR EXCELLENCE IN EDUCATION

Early in 1966, a consultant was hired by the board to prepare the district for integration. Consonant with good principles of community organization, she recommended the establishment of a lay committee that would serve as liaison between the administration and the people of the district, and that would help build a base of support in the community for integration. In the fall of 1966, Citizens for Excellence in Education (CEE) was organized to serve that function. Throughout the struggle, it remained the only significant white integrationist organization in the district.

While it is usually not made explicit, such committees traditionally are expected to perform three valuable services: (1) to legitimate action that the leaders wish to take; (2) to educate the populace for participation in a predetermined and prearranged program; and (3) to provide political support and protection for leaders who would undertake unpopular or controversial programs. On all counts CEE failed. Unlike the leaders of USP, CEE leaders never seriously attempted to establish a mass base. Indeed, they did no serious organizing even among those middle-class liberals who would have been a natural constituency. As the conflict escalated, they did attempt mass meetings, but planing for those meetings was done by a very small group, and community participation was almost nonexistent.

Leadership came almost exclusively from the Kensington-El Cerrito hills and never broadened beyond that area. Unlike USP, whose units in each school provided important links to the people in each neighborhood, CEE was organized along more traditional lines, with a small executive board at the head of a single body which was "the organization." Thus decision-making prerogatives were limited to a few, and

district, losing such neighborhood school strongholds as San Pablo, with 73 percent against him, and Pinole, with 59 percent.

when the rationale for decisions was not self-evident, there were too few out in the community who were ready and able to offer explanations.

Although CEE's initial purpose was to provide liaison between the board and the community, with the irresolution of the liberal board members, more and more energy was devoted to working behind the scenes and keeping informal pressures on the board and administration, and less and less to building a base of support in the community. In fact, it was not until after the liberal majority had promised the district in January 1968 that there would be no two-way busing that CEE made its first serious bid for public attention with an appearance at a board meeting. At that time the organization presented a program to support and facilitate integration and to improve the quality of education in the district.[4] Even at that late date, however, they were still neither organizing nor educating the community effectively. Consequently, at its peak, CEE membership was estimated by its own leaders at no more than five hundred.

While CEE's inability to mobilize a broad constituency was due in part to the structure of the organization, there are two other, perhaps more important, reasons for its ineffectiveness. First, the ambivalence about integration in the white liberal community made many who talked about being for integration unable to make a commitment to the struggle when the issue faced them. Most never became affiliated with the organization. Several CEE leaders complained that even among the membership, most people needed constant reassurance that integration and "excellence in education" were compatible goals. Second, and related to the first, the liberals were divided into moderate and militant camps. This split, which first surfaced in the 1967 election, remained so profound that they were unable to agree upon a single slate of three candidates in 1969, with one group arguing for candidates who would be electable, and the other insisting that principle was paramount and must not be compromised in the interest of electability. Some people said they were disappointed in CEE because it was too radical, too rigid in its advocacy; others, because it was too moderate, too willing to compromise and delay on the implementation of integration.

The roots of this division lay in the fact that the moderates clung to the liberal, pluralist model that sees the society as an amalgam of conflicting groups, and politics as the artful compromise of their competing demands. For the moderates, compromise in the political arena was a basic article of faith, a necessity to ensure the continuity of a valued political system. Given that perspective, they could do nothing but counsel patience, keep talking, and keep hoping that somehow the opposition could be won over, or at least would "get used to the idea." The more militant or radical wing of CEE supporters had by then lost faith in the pluralist image and were pointing insistently to the fact that the minorities and the poor always seemed to get left out of the competition, and arguing that compromise meant continued betrayal of black children and the American promise of equality and freedom.* For them, the only course left was a strong, uncompromising stance.

Complicating the political divisions within CEE was an ambiguity of goals. While believing in integration in principle, the primary goal that drew many people to the organization was its announced focus on excellence in education. For those who organized the group initially — and for most of its leaders throughout its history — excellence in education could not be separated from integration. But for many in the general membership this was not necessarily true, and they needed continual reassurance that integration would not depress the quality of their children's education.

---

* Those who sparked the organization of LACES and the subsequent court action came from this more militant wing of CEE.

That fear made them ambivalent and engendered some sympathy for the wavering of the board's majority.

Together, these factors — the elitism, the board's vacillation, the factionalism, and the ambivalence about integration exhibited by many who were sympathetic in principle — sapped the strength of the integrationist thrust and enfeebled CEE. For USP, on the other hand, all philosophical and political divisions gave way before the threat that their children might be sent to school in the black ghetto. A coalition ranging from moderate to radical right, from working class to middle class was forged around that single issue. It could operate as an effective political force because the differences that divided its membership were submerged in favor of the immediate need to stop the integration of the schools.

THE FINANCIAL SITUATION DETERIORATES

With the near-hysteria about integration, the financial problems of the district were given little attention. As indicated in Chapter 2, after the defeat of their first attempt to increase the tax rate in June 1965, the board consistently refused to act on pleas from teachers, administrators, and some parts of the lay public to put another tax measure before the voters.*

As the financial crisis deepened, program cuts became more drastic, plant maintenance fell behind, books and supplies became scarcer, and teachers' salaries continued to lag

* In the fall of 1968, the local California Teachers Association (CTA) affiliate, the Association of Richmond Educators (ARE), and the Board of Education requested that the Personnel Standards and Ethics Commission (a commission of the CTA, the California School Boards Association, and the California Association of School Administrators) study the RUSD. Its report, issued in November 1968, concluded that the district's financial status was "perilous," a "crisis situation [that] is a direct result of the failure of the communities within the district to achieve a cohesive identity."

behind competitive Bay Area districts. At last, in late 1968 the superintendent warned that without increased taxing power the district might run out of operating funds and have to close the schools. Since that had already happened in other communities across the nation (for example, Youngstown, Ohio), the warning carried a certain plausibility. That, coupled with the fact that the Association of Richmond Educators (ARE) had called a sanctions alert in September, finally galvanized the board into action.* In November 1968 they agreed by a vote of 4–1 to hold an election on February 4, 1969 asking for approval of a $1.50 increase in the tax ceiling.[5] Only Fuller dissented, arguing that $1.00 was all they needed.

The $1.50 proposal stirred the wrath of the black community, the liberals, and the teachers. Terry Hatter, the black former board member who had been defeated in 1967, said that $1.50 was too little and that, in any case, he would neither work nor vote for even that minimal amount unless the board adopted "a meaningful integration plan for the district."[6] The liberals insisted that $1.50 was not nearly enough to cover the financial needs of the schools, that it would only alleviate the immediate crisis, and that the board would have to come back to the people the following year for another increase. The teachers agreed, and ARE, its patience exhausted, invoked sanctions on December 11 and notified teachers and educational institutions throughout the nation of this action.

* Sanctions are a blacklisting device which proclaims to the world that in the professional estimation of its teachers the educational system of a district is seriously deficient and that the district is an unfit place to teach. Sanctions are, according to ARE, "a form of teacher power designed to exert pressure and focus attention upon a school district which through community neglect or inaction has lost or is losing its standing or reputation. They are invoked for the purpose of inducing a reluctant community to improve educational quality, better working conditions, raise pay scales, and in general upgrade poorly supported schools" (ARE *Fact Sheet*, December 1968).

In a panic, the board canceled the scheduled election and shortly thereafter appointed a broad-based citizen study commission to recommend action. Their recommendation (with a strong dissent from the conservative minority on the commission) was that the community be asked to support a tax rate increase of $3.00. The school board's liberal majority offered to compromise for $2.50, the proposal to appear on the April 15 ballot coincident with a school board election in which their seats would be at stake.

The conservatives fought both the $2.50 amount and the April 15 date, contending that $2.50 was too much and April 15 was too soon. They argued that, since the school board election would revolve around the single issue of integration and since the conservatives would not agree to any tax increase so long as any of the money might be spent for busing, the composition of the school board should be known before the people were asked to approve a tax increase. They demanded that the tax rate election come after the school board election so that when voting for increased funds, the people would know who was going to be spending their money. Moreover, they contended that no matter who would assume financial responsibility, $2.50 was far more than the district needed.

The liberals rejected conservative arguments, but this time they could not muster the three votes necessary to win, because one of their number was seriously ill in a Los Angeles hospital. After weeks of bitter argument, the 2–2 stalemate was broken in a dramatic climax. The ailing board member, who had been flown to a Bay Area hospital a few days earlier, was delivered by ambulance to a special meeting and wheeled in on a stretcher to cast the tie-breaking vote. A $2.50 tax-rate increase proposal would be on the April 15 ballot.

CHAPTER 8 **THE ELECTORATE ROARS: 1969**

The divisions within the ranks of the liberals and the unity among the conservatives were soon to make themselves felt again in the electoral process. Several months before the election of April 1969, the liberal board members acknowledged that they were unsure of their chances for reelection and privately indicated a willingness to step down in favor of acceptable alternative candidates. But for the liberals that qualifier "acceptable" was the hitch.

In the fall of 1968, a candidate selection committee, which included representatives of teachers' organizations, white liberals, and blacks, was brought together. No consideration was given to other minority representatives, an oversight that would ultimately further fragment the liberal vote when three Mexican-American candidates entered the race. It was quickly agreed that the blacks would choose one candidate and would make sure that no other black person would run.

The whites almost immediately began to fight over electability *versus* principle, or as one of the more radical participants put it, "Should the candidates go for the center vote and weasel on the issues?" So bitter was the struggle that the black participants eventually withdrew to form their own Black Caucus in order to select their own candidate without being distracted by the fighting among the whites, and also because they had a stake in the outcome of the electability *versus* principle fight and felt they could apply more leverage if they had their own organization. The Black Caucus demanded (and got) the right of veto over selection of the two white candidates, and in a move that surprised the more militant whites but did little to change their minds, came down on the side of electability.

The Black Caucus selected its candidate quickly — Reverend James Smith, a moderate who was well known in the black community. The whites continued to be bitterly divided, however, and by the time the last day for filing declarations of candidacy had arrived, they were still unable to agree. Nevertheless, it was clear that the incumbents had become the embodiment of the integration controversy and could not hope to win. Therefore, on the morning of that last filing day, they held a press conference to announce that they would not stand for reelection and expressed the hope that their removal from the race would facilitate passage of the desperately needed tax increase. By nightfall, fifteen candidates had filed for the three seats — a conservative slate of three, the Black Caucus candidate, and eleven others. Eventually a "unity" slate developed, composed of John Cooper, an attorney; Walter Morgan, a doctor; and James Smith, a minister — all three moderate in their views on integration and busing. But the unity among the liberals was nominal at best.

Meanwhile, the conservatives had organized a slate selection committee that also included various organizations and factions of the right. But they were far less troubled by their philosophical differences. When I asked about that, every respondent who could speak to the question said that no political or ideological differences were felt as keenly as the threat of busing; therefore, they were able to lay aside whatever divisions existed among them. Perhaps, too, it is easier to contain such differences and behave pragmatically in political situations when the scent of victory is caught. And by then, few, if any, still thought the liberals had a chance.

The conservatives knew they would be weakest in the upper-middle-class Kensington and El Cerrito hills area, and several said they spent considerable time trying to find a professional from that neighborhood who would agree to run. Eventually William Jageman, a Kensington attorney, joined the slate, which included Don Bartels, a real estate agent, and James Shattuck, the first president of USP, who worked at the repair and maintenance of heating and refrigeration equipment.

The conservative campaign that followed was a smooth, well run operation, well financed and never short of volunteers. Their catchy slogan, "Education Not Buses," was used very effectively in the media and allowed people to avert their gaze from the racism implicit in the campaign. So well did it go that one campaign co-chairman said,

> Most campaigns never have enough money, never have enough workers. This one had both money and volunteers coming out of my ears. We had an enormous amount of professional time donated and material given to us at cost or below — about $5,000 or $6,000 worth. In cash we raised and spent about $18,000 or so more.

The financial statements filed by the conservative candidates after the election showed that almost $19,000 had been raised in the campaign, with large contributions coming from prominent members of Richmond's business community, many of whom had formerly taken more moderate positions.*

USP's grass roots organizing paid off handsomely; their volunteers staffed the campaign headquarters, walked almost every white precinct in the district, mounted a tremendous telephone campaign, raised money, and kept the pressure on the local press (which was swamped by both visits and letters to the editor) and on their city governments.

As the pressure mounted, the *Richmond Independent* fell into line. By February 11, in an editorial titled "There Is 'No Such Law of the Land,'" its editors reversed the position they had taken just three months earlier when they had urged their readers to accept the Verde plan because the conditions at Verde were "in violation of the Civil Rights bill and the Supreme Court ruling on integration." They now argued:

> . . . the United States Supreme Court has never ruled there must be integration, much less that racial balance must be corrected, when segregation is the result of normal conditions and constitutes no deliberate act of discrimination by a public agency.

When, on April 12, the *Independent* also endorsed the neighborhood schools candidates, the newspaper had moved to a point diametrically opposed to its earlier pro-integration stance.

The integrationists' campaign limped along with little money and few volunteers. Their joint statement of campaign expenditures shows that just a little more than $12,000

---

* Among these contributors were the Western Contra Costa County Board of Realtors, ranking executives in the Richmond Chamber of Commerce and the Richmond-based Mechanics Bank, and other members of Richmond's banking, commercial, and industrial world. (Source: Contra Costa County Superintendent of Schools.)

was spent.[1] There was little positive affect and enthusiasm for the unity slate of Cooper, Morgan, and Smith. The campaign was largely without passion or commitment. It was not enough that many people ardently detested the conservative slate and all that they stood for. As anyone who has been close to a local political campaign knows, in order to sell the rest of the people, those involved in the campaign must be thoroughly and absolutely committed to their candidate. Unfortunately for the liberal slate, this was not true of their supporters.

The outline of the integrationists' defeat was clear within an hour after the polls closed on election day; only the magnitude was in doubt. Turnout had been unusually heavy for a local election (67 percent), with some of the precincts where sentiment against integration was heaviest turning out more than 80 percent of the vote.* A joyous tumult reigned in conservative headquarters throughout the long evening of the vote counting; the liberal headquarters was sunk in gloom. When the night was over, the liberals had been overwhelmingly defeated — the three conservative candidates polling 91,000 votes and the liberals 37,000.

Examination of Table 11 shows that the anti-integrationists won by 2.5–1. Among white voters, the city of San Pablo and the unincorporated areas of El Sobrante, Giant, and Rollingwood (all dominantly white working-class communities) gave the conservatives their largest majorities, ranging from 86 percent to 92 percent. Pinole, a dominantly lower-middle-class and working-class city, gave them more than 83 percent. In fact, the anti-integrationists suffered

---

* Compare the turnout in the 1969 election to that in 1967 when it was 37 percent — an increase of 81 percent in two years, and a good indication of how high fears and passions had risen. Recall that in 1967 anti-busing leaders reported that they were fighting to arouse a public that was uninformed and relatively unconcerned. By 1969, two years of controversy had made their mark on the public consciousness.

Table 11. Results of the RUSD School Board
and Tax Rate Election, April 15, 1969

Community	Candidates[a]			Tax Rate Increase	
	Liberal	Conservative	Other	Yes	No
Cities					
Richmond	34.2%	59.2%	6.6%	42.7%	57.3%
	(19,217)	(33,286)	(3,682)	(7,914)	(10,600)
El Cerrito	33.0	62.0	5.0	46.3	53.7
	(8,751)	(16,423)	(1,315)	(4,151)	(4,810)
Hercules	15.8	76.0	7.3	35.3	64.7
	(41)	(200)	(19)	(30)	(55)
Pinole	13.4	83.2	3.4	31.6	68.4
	(1,490)	(9,278)	(378)	(1,231)	(2,662)
San Pablo	8.5	86.2	5.3	20.7	79.3
	(841)	(8,575)	(526)	(686)	(2,632)
Unincorporated Areas					
Kensington	49.0	48.4	2.6	62.6	37.4
	(4,015)	(3,969)	(215)	(1,721)	(1,029)
East Richmond	24.5	71.5	4.0	40.3	59.7
	(1,244)	(3,631)	(204)	(684)	(1,016)
El Sobrante	10.6	86.4	3.0	23.3	76.7
	(825)	(6,703)	(229)	(601)	(1,978)
Rollingwood	7.4	86.7	5.9	37.1	62.9
	(140)	(1,636)	(112)	(283)	(479)
Giant	5.8	92.2	2.0	21.4	78.6
	(467)	(7,399)	(164)	(572)	(2,106)
TOTAL	27.4%	67.5%	5.1%	39.5%	60.5%
	(37,031)	(91,100)	(6,844)	(17,873)	(27,367)

SOURCE: Computed from data of the Contra Costa County Registration-Election Department, Martinez.

[a] The difference in the total number of votes recorded for the school board and tax increase is due to the fact that voters were asked to vote for three candidates in the school board race.

their only defeat among white voters in the Kensington-El Cerrito hills which the integrationists carried by a very slim margin.

At the same time, the $2.50 tax rate increase proposal was defeated 3–2. Although it had been twice endorsed by the *Independent*,[2] although the Richmond Chamber of

Commerce had unequivocally recommended its support,[3] and although last minute scare headlines appeared in the *Independent* warning, "Richmond Near School Collapse,"[4] 60.4 percent of the voters said no. Table 11 shows that the proposal lost in every white community in the district but Kensington.

Both the integrationist school board candidates and the tax rate increase fared best in the black community. There are nine dominantly black precincts in the district, all located in Richmond's Black Crescent. The integration slate carried those precincts by almost 83 percent, compared to the seven Kensington-El Cerrito hills precincts which expressed their ambivalence by splitting almost 50–50, giving only a slight edge to the integrationists.* The tax proposal in the same black precincts won by almost 74 percent, compared to only 63 percent in the upper-middle-class hills precincts.†

It is difficult to know why the tax proposal did so much better in the black community than in the hills; or why, in fact, the black community has supported every tax and bond election in the district's history. My first guess was that the difference was because there were fewer homeowners in black neighborhoods. But a look at the results in Par-

* Despite the conservative landslide, Jageman, the Kensington attorney who had been counted on to make the conservative slate respectable in the hills, did not carry his own precinct. It went to the integration slate with 55.3 percent, the highest vote with which they carried any white precinct in the district.

† In the only other precinct in the district that can be classified as upper-middle-class in terms of income, a newly developed neighborhood in Pinole, the tax proposal was soundly defeated by a vote of 566 to 346, or more than 62 percent against, and the conservative candidates carried with about 82 percent. This lends credence to my notion that income alone was not a predictor of voting behavior and that the liberal, cosmopolitan, professional upper-middle-class life style of the hills population, heavily influenced by university-related families, was the critical variable.

chester Village, a relatively poor, black, homeowning section, does not bear out that hunch. There, the tax proposal won overwhelmingly by a vote of 237 to 55, or better than 81 percent. Two other black precincts where homeowning rates are high gave the proposal more than 77 percent of the vote.

Perhaps blacks vote for higher school taxes because they still have some faith that if there is more money, their schools will get a larger share. Whatever the reason, if we assume that a vote to increase school taxes is some small measure of the value one places on education, then these facts do not support the racial stereotype that tells us that black children do poorly in school because their parents do not value education.

Table 12, using sample precincts in each of seven socioeconomic areas,[5] shows the almost perfect correlation between SES and voter turnout, with the black Areas 1 and 2 the lowest, and the upper-middle-class hills Area 7, the highest. Only Area 6 failed to conform to the pattern. This irregularity may be explained by the fact that the area itself, Point Richmond, is an anomaly embracing both a professional upper-middle-class population who live in homes right on the bay, and a poor working-class population, some of whom still make their living by fishing.

This table also shows the district-wide correlation between the candidates and the tax increase vote. Again, only area 6 shows a reversal. There, the integration candidate received only about 35 percent of the vote, while the tax measure carried narrowly with just under 51 percent.

TWO COMPARISONS

Proposition 14

Since the neighborhood schools advocates argued loudly that they did not oppose integration but only busing, and since they insisted that the pattern of school segrega-

Table 12. Vote on RUSD School Board and
Tax Rate Increase, by Sample Precincts,
April 15, 1969

Social Area[a]	Precinct	Total Vote	Percent Turnout	School Board			Tax Rate	
				Liberal	Conservative	Other	Yes	No
Area 1	220 236 255	3,721	53.8%	81.7% (3,039)	8.1% (300)	10.2% (382)	76.5% (832)	23.5% (255)
Area 2	189 194 197	4,655	56.7	80.9 (3,821)	8.9 (412)	9.1 (422)	70.8 (1,035)	29.2 (426)
Area 3	228 238 256	5,394	66.2	8.1 (435)	87.5 (4,718)	4.4 (241)	22.7 (409)	77.3 (1,393)
Area 4	252 253 261	5,776	73.4	9.9 (571)	87.1 (5,031)	3.0 (174)	21.9 (422)	78.1 (1,505)
Area 5	208 257 259	6,269	73.4	9.8 (612)	87.2 (5,470)	3.0 (187)	24.2 (508)	75.8 (1,589)
Area 6	187 188	1,937	62.7	34.8 (674)	54.6 (1,058)	10.6 (205)	50.8 (332)	49.2 (332)
Area 7	214 217	4,958	73.6	51.5 (2,551)	45.4 (2,252)	3.1 (155)	65.6 (1,089)	34.4 (571)

[a] The seven social areas used here are taken from Alan B. Wilson, *Western Contra Costa County Population, 1965. Demographic Characteristics.* The three major variables underlying this classification are race, socioeconomic status, and social disorganization. Indices of social disorganization are unemployment, broken families, and dilapidated or crowded housing. Areas 1 and 2 are predominantly black, with low SES and high social disorganization. The rest are predominantly white. Area 3 exhibits low SES and high social disorganization. Areas 4 and 5 are medium in SES, with little and moderate social disorganization, respectively. Area 6 is heterogeneous in SES, with high social disorganization. Area 7 has high SES and low social disorganization.

tion was simply an artifact of residential segregation in which they bore no responsibility, it seemed interesting to compare the 1969 school board vote in the RUSD with the 1964 vote for Proposition 14, a statewide measure that sought (successfully, although it was later overturned in the courts) to retain the right to discriminate in the sale and rental of housing in California. A "yes" vote was a vote for housing discrimination.

Table 13 shows that comparison. Only Kensington failed to support the proposition; its 1964 vote compares quite closely to its 1969 vote. In fact, the votes on the two issues were surprisingly stable in all the communities in the district. El Cerrito alone showed a slight drop in the anti-integration vote between 1964 and 1969; all the other communities showed slight increases. In both schools and housing the anti-integrationists were a substantial majority.

In 1964 the rallying cry of the proponents of Proposi-

Table 13. Comparison of the RUSD 1969 School Board Election and the Vote for Proposition 14 in 1964

| Area | School Board | | | Proposition 14 | |
	Liberal	Conservative	Other	No	Yes[a]
Kensington	49.1%	48.3%	2.6%	52.7%	47.3%
	(4,025)	(3,969)	(215)	(1,551)	(1,393)
Richmond	34.2	59.2	6.6	43.9	56.1
	(19,217)	(33,286)	(3,682)	(12,657)	(16,179)
El Cerrito	32.9	62.2	4.9	35.1	64.9
	(8,751)	(16,523)	(1,315)	(4,123)	(7,626)
Hercules	15.8	76.9	7.3	27.6	72.4
	(41)	(200)	(19)	(42)	(110)
Pinole	12.8	83.9	3.3	23.4	76.6
	(1,490)	(9,728)	(378)	(772)	(2,526)
San Pablo	8.5	86.2	5.3	22.6	77.4
	(841)	(8,575)	(526)	(1,489)	(5,102)

SOURCE: Compiled from voting records of the Contra Costa County Registration-Election Department, Martinez

[a] A yes vote favored discrimination in housing.

tion 14 was that any restriction on the right to sell or rent a house to whomever one pleased was an abridgement of freedom and liberty. Curious about how my conservative respondents had felt then and whether they had changed in the intervening six years, I asked several to talk about it. One reply, selected because it is typical, follows:

> If I owned property I wouldn't want the law to tell me I had to rent to some guy just because he's black. It's an infringement on my rights and my property . . . I don't care what color he is, it's my right to make judgments about who should live on my property.

Thus, they argued that their stand on neighborhood schools had nothing to do with race; they pleaded not to be called racists; they insisted that the problem was due only to housing segregation over which they had no control, but every anti-busing person I asked admitted that he had voted for Proposition 14, and none indicated that he would change that vote if confronted with the same issue again.

Wallace for President: 1968

Another indicator of racist sentiments, the 1968 vote for George Wallace, also provides an illuminating comparison. In an election in which he captured just under 12 percent of the votes in the state and just over 8 percent of the votes in Contra Costa County, the working-class and lower-middle-class communities in the RUSD voted for him in considerably heavier numbers. San Pablo gave him 21.7 percent, the highest Wallace vote in any community in the state. The Pinole-Giant * area cast 19.1 percent of its votes

---

* Giant is an unincorporated, largely working-class area adjoining Pinole. Together with San Pablo, it formed the most articulate center of resistance to integration. Two members of the current school board and most of USP's active leaders live there.

for Wallace, and El Sobrante, 15.1 percent. El Cerrito, which includes both a working-class flatlands area and an upper-middle-class hills section, voted at about the county average — 8.2 percent. Compare these figures with Kensington which gave him only 2.4 percent.*

The pattern is the same. If the Wallace vote is taken as an indicator of racism, that sentiment is highest in those areas where the 1969 vote against integration was also highest.

In sum, except for the magnitude of the liberal defeat, the election results were predictable. The liberals' ambivalent commitments, their divided forces, the strength of America's racial fears and hostilities, and the liberals' inability to offer any payoff that might have encouraged people to overcome those fears, all assured their failure.

---

* The upper-middle-class suburbs in the eastern section of the county were equally indifferent to the Wallace appeal. Only 2.7 percent of the voters in Orinda cast ballots for Wallace, 2.9 percent in Moraga, and 3.6 percent in Lafayette.

PART FOUR

AFTERMATH

CHAPTER 9

**THE LAME DUCK
BOARD**

Once defeated, there was nothing left to lose, and the lame-duck board members were released from the constraints that had previously bound them. Two important things were yet to be done, and they were determined to do them. One was to place another tax proposal before the voters; the other, to set the stage for the implementation of their busing plan.

ANOTHER TAX-RATE PROPOSAL

On April 16, the day after the election, the board set a new tax rate increase election. Usp spokesmen and the board members-elect insisted on a $1.50 proposal, while the defeated liberals, in a striking display of insensitivity to the implications of their defeat, argued that $1.93 was the necessary minimum and insisted that they would accept no less. A usp spokesman reminded the liberals that whereas they still had a 3-2 majority, the election results should have made clear that they could not pass a tax election without USP support. The conservatives demanded, therefore, that the board establish a rate satisfactory to USP. The board president replied that USP must realize that the support of the whole community was needed to pass a tax election. The triumphant response from the large conservative audience was spontaneous and electric. "We *are* the community!" they shouted with almost a single voice.

After hours of haggling and shouting, the liberals agreed to a proposal requesting $1.50, the election to be held on the earliest date legally permissible, July 8, 1969.*

Except for CEE, the white community was solidly behind the new tax proposal. Standard Oil donated $1,000 to the campaign. The powerful Richmond Council of Industries was vocal in its support. Both local teacher organizations endorsed the measure. The Richmond Federation of Teachers gave only nominal support; ARE which had brought sanctions down on the district four months earlier in anger over a similar proposal, reluctantly endorsed this one.†

Only CEE refused to back the proposal, holding firmly to its position that $1.50 was inadequate to meet basic educational needs. In addition, CEE argued that it was the responsibility of those who had used their "strength and organizational discipline to defeat the April tax increase to use those same assets to pass the lesser amount in July." [1] Some CEE members were outraged by this position, and it further fragmented the liberal community.

---

* Earlier I indicated that the law does not permit any tax funds approved after the beginning of the fiscal year (July 1) to be used in that year. Due to the desperate financial situation in the district, however, the County Board of Education lifted that restriction.

† ARE moved to lift sanctions almost immediately after the proposal passed despite the fact that none of their complaints about educational quality or segregated schools were ameliorated. Indeed, the only change was that the teachers got their raises.

In the black community, word was passed quietly at first to vote no. But fearful that the quiet tactic was not enough, about two weeks before the election a mailing went to residents of the black community asking them to vote against the tax rate proposal because of racism in the schools and in the newly elected board. Among the signers of the letter were many in Richmond's black "establishment" and several people connected with the school system — a black principal, several black teachers, and several school community workers.*

The bitterness of the years just past and the election campaign just fought was carried over into the new campaign. Whereas in the April tax election the liberals had appealed without success to the conservative conscience "for the sake of the children," now the situation was reversed. Whereas in April a conservative leader had said they would "never vote one cent to people who would use money to bus our children," the same speaker now condemned the liberals for being unwilling to vote money to those who would *not* bus children.

> They said they'd rather see it go down to defeat than to give money to be used in ways that they don't approve of. Can you imagine that? They just don't care about the children at all.

But the conservatives had been successful in mobilizing opposition to the April tax election because their constituency was poorer and therefore more likely to feel the pinch of increased taxes; and because they believed there were already too many frills in the system. Together, these

* The school community workers were not rehired the next fall (see Chapter 10), and the black principal — a man who would seem like a moderate in many urban communities today, but who in Richmond was considered a flaming militant — left the district to become the principal of a school in Berkeley, charging that he had been forced out of his job because of his political activities.

two factors enabled many working-class and lower-middle-class people to vote against the tax proposal without pangs of conscience. The upper-middle class, on the other hand, historically has been willing and able to pay for education. Its members can suffer tax increases with less pain, and for them there are not enough "frills"; any decrease in program or staff seems catastrophic. Thus, many who did not want to support the conservative board could not translate that reluctance into a vote against school taxes; it seemed almost a sacrilege.

Consequently, the tax proposal carried by a slim 1,706 votes out of 31,417 cast, for a majority of less than 53 percent. Only about 43 percent of the voters went to the polls in July, compared to 67 percent in April.

Table 14 compares the April and July votes in the same precincts which were analyzed in Table 12. Notice that although the shift to support of the tax proposal in the working-class and lower-middle-class areas is striking, the boast of the USP president that the organization could deliver its constituency in support of the new tax measure as solidly as it had voted against the previous one was not borne out by the election results. In fact, in Area 3, a USP stronghold in San Pablo and north-central Richmond, the measure failed by a substantial majority — 65 percent. And the home precinct of the USP president (#238) voted heavily against the proposal, an indication that people often vote their pocketbooks and convictions on school financing regardless of exhortations and appeals from those claiming to be their leaders.

Areas 1 and 2, in the black community, show that black voters almost completely reversed themselves between April and July, a strikingly sophisticated and self-interested vote. In the April election, with an integrated school system still a potential, black voters overwhelmingly supported

Table 14. RUSD Tax Rate Elections, April 15
and July 8, 1968, by Sample Precincts

Social Area[a]	Pre-cinct	April 15			July 8		
		Yes	No	Percent Turnout	Yes	No	Percent Turnout
	220						
Area 1	236	76.5%	23.5%	53.8%	30.1%	69.9%	30.4%
	255	(832)	(255)		(231)	(536)	
	189						
Area 2	194	70.9	29.1	56.7	29.1	70.9	30.3
	197	(1,035)	(426)		(263)	(642)	
	228						
Area 3	238	22.7	77.3	66.2	44.4	55.6	39.2
	256	(409)	(1,393)		(486)	(609)	
	252						
Area 4	253	21.9	78.1	73.4	52.3	47.7	39.6
	261	(422)	(1,505)		(546)	(497)	
	208						
Area 5	257	24.2	75.8	73.4	59.3	40.7	41.0
	259	(508)	(1,589)		(762)	(524)	
	187	50.8	49.2	62.7	54.3	45.7	39.1
Area 6	188	(332)	(322)		(226)	(190)	
	214	65.6	34.4	73.6	64.6	35.4	47.2
Area 7	217	(1,089)	(571)		(695)	(381)	

[a] The seven social areas are taken from Alan B. Wilson, *Western Contra Costa County Population, 1965. Demographic Characteristics.* The three major variables underlying this classification are race, socioeconomic status, and social disorganization. Indices of social disorganization are unemployment, broken families, and dilapidated or crowded housing. Areas 1 and 2 are predominantly black, with low SES and high social disorganization. The rest are predominantly white. Area 3 exhibits low SES and high social disorganization. Areas 4 and 5 are medium in SES, with little and moderate social disorganization, respectively. Area 6 is heterogeneous in SES, with high social disorganization. Area 7 has high SES and low social disorganization.

a $2.50 tax increase. In July, when integration was dead, they refused to give their adversaries even $1.50.

Area 7, in the Kensington-El Cerrito hills, had the

highest turnout — just over 47 percent — and supported the tax increase by more than 64 percent. But notice that the July election drew about 26 percent fewer voters from those hills precincts to the polls, a striking drop-off in an area where turnout has always been high. Unable to bring themselves to vote against a school tax increase, yet unwilling to cast a ballot that seemed to support the conservative board, the white, hill liberals stayed home in extraordinary numbers. Blacks, too, voted in considerably smaller numbers, with Areas 1 and 2 turning out at just over 30 percent, compared to almost 54 percent and 57 percent respectively in April. By staying home, they lost their only bargaining tool with the conservative board. For if the tax election had been defeated by a coalition of blacks and integrationist white liberals — an easy possibility since they needed only 1,706 votes and together these areas sent 3,752 fewer voters to the polls in July than in April — the cost of failing to consider their demands would have been borne home dramatically to the newly elected board. Desperate for money, they would have been forced to deal with the liberals and the blacks. As it was, the conservatives saw the liberals as politically impotent — a paper tiger — and secure in the knowledge that they need fear no political ɹepercussions, they were free to pursue their own course.

IMPLEMENTING PHASE 1

Throughout the weeks after their defeat, the lame-duck liberals continued to present plans for the implementation of Phase 1, while their conservative colleagues offered intense objections. Conservative rage was so high that several times administrative spokesmen who were presenting the plans before the school board were hooted and shouted down. Finally, on May 12, just six weeks before they would leave office, the liberals adopted new elementary school boundaries for the purpose of implementing the first phase of the three-stage integration plan.

The conservatives, of course, protested vigorously that the board was not responding to the will of the people as demonstrated in the April 15 election. The liberals replied that they were responding to the law of the land. The conservatives charged that this was a liberal scheme to set the district up for a desegregation suit. They feared that after they took office and rescinded these boundary changes, the Legal Services Foundation would seek an injunction to halt their action, claiming that the conservative board was returning the boundaries to their former lines in order to perpetuate segregation. The board president did not deny these allegations. Indeed, his farewell address to the district indicated that that was precisely what his intention had been.[2]

> The future of the district lies in the courts . . . . The new board will be forced to implement what we've done. We have here a *fait accompli*. We have changed the school boundaries to reflect an integrated district, and any attempt to change it back will wind up in a lawsuit.

A top leader of CEE confirmed this statement when he said that "the board redrew the boundaries at our insistence to lay the basis for a lawsuit."

In sum, the tax victory meant that the new board could begin its work on a note of triumph and relieved of the terrible financial pressures under which the district had been operating for some time. It also meant that the teachers could have their raises and that the sanctions against the district would be lifted. As for integration, the prospect was dim under any circumstances, and considerably dimmer after the tax victory which had convinced the conservatives that they needed neither the liberals nor the blacks to carry on the business of the district.

10 **CONSERVATIVES TAKE OFFICE**

With their ascension to power, the conservatives were in a position to realize their two major goals: to stop integration, and to remold the educational system to suit their idealized image. In part because of their political philosophy which dealt in absolutes, in part because of their constricted experience in community participation which left them relatively free from political and social cross-pressures, the new men of power were neither compromisers nor conciliators. In addition, their smashing political victory in April and the passage of the tax election in July made them feel invulnerable to any political threats from their adversaries. Hence, there was little need for constraint on their part.

As the time approached for the conservatives to take office, at least one political adviser counseled them against any immediate action that would stir the liberal wrath.

I tried to convince the new board to put off any action that would undo what the liberal board did — that is, firing Widel and rescinding Phase 1 — until after the July tax election. I was really frightened that it would lose whatever liberal support we might get for the tax election if they took those actions on July 1, and I couldn't see any reason why they couldn't put them off for a week.

But USP leaders argued that the symbols of their travail could not be permitted to stand an extra week. To accede to any delay was to forestall tasting the fruits of victory.

PHASE 1 IS SUSPENDED

At their first meeting on July 1, the conservative board ousted Denzil Widel, the superintendent of schools and elevated in his stead the deputy superintendent, Woodrow Wilson Snodgrass, a local man who had grown up in Richmond, had graduated from Richmond High School, and had made his way up through the ranks of Richmond's educational hierarchy over the past thirty-five years. He was deeply tied into the administrative bureaucracy. As one respondent said,

The schools in Richmond are run by a small professional "club" — an entrenched group who have been there for many years. They're all local people; they all went to Richmond High together; they used to work together at El Cerrito High; and now they've fanned out into many of the top administrative posts. They have a tight-knit little clique that can subvert any program they want to.

In addition, Snodgrass was a trusted conservative who had won further favor by his covert opposition to the liberal Widel and by his overt stance against busing. Several liberals believed that Snodgrass had subverted the former administration. He was often accused of "manipulating the bureaucracy" with which he was so familiar. One former board member said bitterly,

He double crossed and worked against both the board and
the superintendent. When he was given the task of redrawing
the boundaries at Portola [Junior High School] in order to
effect racial balance in that school, he did it so that some
children who live almost next door to Portola had to travel
across town to Adams. The plan was a total disaster and
helped to crystallize public opinion against redrawing school
boundary lines. He knows this district better than anyone
else, so it wasn't just an innocent mistake. He did it to subvert
integration.*

With a new chief administrator acting as secretary of
the board, the board members quickly suspended Phase 1
of the three-year integration plan and ordered Snodgrass
to "submit alternate plans that do not include forced busing
of children for racial balance."[1] Within a week the district
announced its alternative proposal, an open enrollment plan
heralded as district-wide, in which students were given the
option of attending one of a cluster of schools. The plan was
quite simple: for each black school there were two, three,
or four white schools that made up the open enrollment
cluster. Within that cluster any black child might choose
any white school, and any white child might go to the black
school. No transfers were to be permitted from one white
school to another. Any participating student would be transported to and from the school of his choice at district
expense.†

It is interesting, however, that six schools in the north
end of the district where resistance to desegregation was
most intense,‡ were not included in any of the open enroll-

---

* When I asked Widel whether he shared this view, he said sadly,
"I guess he did what he thought was best from his frame of reference. But I must say, that was a serious mistake to give him that
job."

† See Appendix, Documents 2 and 3, showing the areas of open
enrollment and the rules governing the plan.

‡ The schools were Tara Hills, Kerry Hills, Shannon, Ellerhorst,

ment clusters. District officials contend that it is scurrilous to bring this up. The reason for the omission, they say, is simply that the schools were already overcrowded. But many find that explanation less than persuasive since other schools in the district had space problems as well. Moreover, in several of these schools, portable classrooms had been brought in to handle the increasing enrollment of white children. The district's critics asked, "Why not for blacks?" The reason, I believe, was that since the conservative sweep, racial attitudes in these areas had hardened once again; resistance to having black children in their white schools was no longer a socially unacceptable position.

As the conservatives had predicted, within days after the suspension of Phase 1, the Legal Services Foundation, on behalf of their clients, petitioned the court to enjoin the board from rescinding the desegregation plan. On July 28, just one week before the start of the first open enrollment period, a Superior Court judge ruled that, despite all indications that open enrollment plans did not and would not work, the district should have a chance to prove that its plan constituted adequate compliance with the law. He gave the district one year, until May 20, 1970, to demonstrate the feasibility of its open enrollment plan.

By the end of the open enrollment period (August 15) only 452 students at all elementary and secondary school levels had chosen to transfer; most of them were black students moving to white schools. The open enrollment period was extended, but, even so, only a little more than 1,000 students (out of 41,367, of whom 10,615 were black) were involved in the first year.

In a series of delaying tactics, the district has managed

Montalvin Manor, and El Sobrante, all with between 0 and 2 percent black population. These schools provided the leadership for the conservative drive to victory. Three of the five board members and most of USP's leadership had children in one or another of them.

postponement after postponement in the courts, so that the open enrollment plan continues unchanged into the 1971/1972 school year. As of October 1971 another 500 students (again mostly black) chose to participate, putting the number of students involved, after three years, at about 1,500.

In sum, open enrollment has done nothing to change the racial balance in the nine ghetto schools.* At best, open enrollment has succeeded in enhancing somewhat the racial balance in schools that were formerly predominantly white, in helping to spread about 1,500 more black students around the district, and in somewhat alleviating the desperate overcrowding in the dominantly black schools. But the ghetto schools remain almost all black and, in fact, have increased their black populations by a few percentage points.

THE CONSERVATIVE BOARD INSULATES ITSELF

Its two most urgent priorities accomplished — the firing of the superintendent and the suspension of the integration plan — the board settled down to a lengthy discussion on ways to "speed up" and "shorten" board meetings. Members suggested the curtailment of either the number of speakers they would hear on an issue or the length of time they would be permitted to speak, or both. This board, which throughout the liberal reign had railed that democracy was threatened if debate were cut off, these men (one of whom had walked out of a meeting a few months earlier when the liberal chairman had ruled him out of order) now sought to control the opposition by limiting debate and confining the circumstances under which people could be heard. The new president — the most articulate defender of his constituents' right to debate any issue for any length of time when he was a member of the minority — now solemnly reminded the assemblage: "A board meeting is not a public forum. It is held to administer the business of the district."

* See Table 9, for testimony to this.

While no decision was made at that meeting, the board eventually did develop procedures which helped to insulate the members from public pressure. First, in order to secure a place on the agenda, the board required that a request be made in writing five working days before a meeting and that the applicant must specify exactly what he wished to address the board about. The administration justifies the time and specificity requirement with the argument that it permits them to gather data for an intelligent response. In practice, however, the procedure often serves as a device for discouraging participation and for screening out or stalling individuals or groups the board prefers not to hear.

For example, when CEE requested time on the agenda to address the board on its open enrollment policy, the organization was put off for months. The first excuse was that CEE had not met the five-day notice requirement. My informant explained,

> I did get the notice to them on the Wednesday before the next Wednesday's meeting, but it turned out that there weren't five *working days*, since one of the days in that week was a school holiday.

Having corrected that problem the next month, the request was turned down again because "[The administration] said that I hadn't specified in sufficient detail what my presentation would say." And so it went for three months. It takes determination and persistence to continue in the face of such administrative perversity.

Even so respectable an organization as the West Contra Costa Council of PTA was stalled for months when it requested time to address the board on the subject of student representation on the school board. After hurdling the bureaucratic roadblocks around time and specificity, the PTA was told simply that, since no one on the board thought it a good idea to have students sit with them, there was nothing to discuss. Only dogged insistence on a public hearing finally got time on the agenda for the PTA after months of hassle and delay.

Second, once on the agenda, strict time limitations are imposed upon discussants: an individual is permitted two minutes to speak, and an organization is given five minutes. Time is kept by one of the administrators who controls a small signal light (much like a miniature traffic light) which is positioned where the board can see it clearly. The signal is green when a speaker begins, flashes a warning yellow when he has fifteen seconds left, and turns red when his time is up. If the speaker is not a friend of the board, no leeway is given; the chairman cuts him off almost instantly.

These two mechanisms, together with a chairman who wields his gavel dictatorially when his opponents are on the floor, have intimidated a great many people. Responding to my question about why they were no longer heard from regularly at board meetings, one black informant said,

> No one wants to subject himself to that. We'd be on the agenda, and most of the time they'd never get to us. Or if they did, our spokesman would be called out of order, or out of time, or they'd just shut him off. Or else Mr. Fuller would be just plain nasty. Or they wouldn't respond to anything we said. They'd just sit there and as soon as we were finished, they'd go on to the next item of business.

Notice how eloquently this statement outlines the tactics of the conservative board, and how corrosive such tactics are to morale. One need never actually deny the opportunity to speak. Delay, obfuscation, and ignoring people when they speak accomplish the same goal quite effectively.

Furthermore, this board has an extraordinary record of missed meetings and executive sessions (closed-door sessions in which only the action taken is affirmed in public).

In their first full year in office (July 1969–June 1970), they cancelled six meetings (25 percent of the total number regularly scheduled in a year). In the previous year, when the liberal majority made the decisions, not a single meeting was canceled. Most cancellations have been on short public notice — rarely more than two days — and unless one has a very sharp eye out for school news in the *Richmond Independent*, very easy to miss. More than once, people gathered at the regularly appointed time and place only to find that the meeting had been canceled with the only public notice being an announcement buried somewhere on the pages of the *Independent* a day or two earlier (once, on the very night of the meeting).

It is a little more difficult to compare precisely the number of executive sessions the two boards held, since the 1968/1969 record is not absolutely clear.* But leaving out the routine sessions concerning personnel matters which school boards normally hold either before or after regular sessions, the conservatives held twelve special executive sessions, some lasting as long as four or five hours. In addition, almost every meeting either began or ended with an executive session. Often no action was affirmed in public session because, it was announced, none was taken. Therefore, the subject of many such meetings was never made known publicly. By comparison, there is no record that the liberals ever held so many or such lengthy executive sessions. Indeed, apart from the routine personnel meetings, there is evidence of only three special executive meetings

* The question of executive sessions is relevant because many in the district believe that the board uses them to circumvent the Brown Act, which makes it illegal for a quorum of a school board to gather in anything but a public session which has been given adequate public notice except under specific conditions, for example, for the purpose of discussing personnel, litigation, or hearings on student discipline.

during the 1968/1969 school year. One former board member commented on the conservatives' record:

> There just isn't any reason for so many executive sessions. There's certainly no reason for such a meeting at the beginning of every board meeting as this board does. When we did have executive sessions, we were always very careful to explain what they were about.

The conservatives reply to these criticisms that their many executive sessions are necessary because of the litigation in which the district is involved. But the liberal board managed also to sustain many lawsuits, including the Verde Suit, without so much secrecy.

THE OPPOSITION IS SCORNED

A discussion of a drug-abuse program for the schools provides a typical example of the scorn with which a liberal spokesman is treated by the conservative board. The drug units of the various city police departments within the district presented their viewpoints. When the board settled down to discuss a motion about the adoption of the proposed drug-abuse program, a young lawyer rose to ask whether the program would present perspectives about the drug problem other than those held by law enforcement agencies. "Would some of the acknowledged medical experts be heard?" he asked. The board president, his voice registering incredulity, replied, "Are you FOR drug abuse, Mr. Peppard?" Peppard, angrily, "Of course not; that's not the point. All I want to know is whether there will be provision for other views to be heard even when they diverge from the law enforcement view." The board president, scornfully, "No, Mr. Peppard, we will not allow you or anyone else to come before our students to speak in favor of drug abuse."

Nor is any quarter given to the black community. Long

hostile to the school community worker program, a state and federally funded program that puts minority laymen into the schools to serve as paraprofessionals and to provide links between school and community, the conservatives failed to rehire four of the most militant blacks among them. The school board and administration charged the community workers with incompetence. A federal judge did not agree. In response to a suit brought by the discharged employees, he ruled that the RUSD had to rehire them since they had established a *prima facie* case that they had been discharged for participating actively in the school board and tax elections. The board threatened to appeal the decision, but two years later it still had not done so, indicating that school district attorneys saw little chance of reversal.

But the conservatives eventually had their way, for in the 1970/1971 budget, these teachers' aides were reduced in number from 124 to 41. When the cutback was challenged, the board explained that it was necessary because it did not know how much state and federal funding would be available. A spokesman for the black community asked the board if it would rehire the aides up to the previous year's strength if and when the money became available. Fifteen minutes later the board was still temporizing, and the petitioner was still saying, "Just give me a simple yes or no answer." Finally one member, James Shattuck, agreed that they were, indeed, talking around the question and said, "No! We will not make that commitment. This school board is not in a position to say now that we will use any part of any new money to hire teachers' aides." Fuller concurred vocally, while the rest of the board implicitly accepted the statement by their silence. The angry black man replied, "This meeting began with a discussion of what to do about Nystrom [a ghetto school that had been damaged by arson a few days earlier] and how to deal with such problems. Well, I don't think this board cares at all about Ny-

strom, and we now know that and what to do about it."
Shattuck responded angrily, "I might say that the money
that was spent last year wasn't that helpful obviously."

The USP leaders with whom I was sitting at that meeting all giggled appreciatively at Shattuck's retort, and one
muttered, "Thatta boy! Get tough with 'em." Their tension
throughout the exchange was palpable. From the time the
black man appeared at the microphone, their disdain and
hostility were clearly visible, not only in their under-the-
breath comments (such as, "What in hell do they want now?
Always asking for something for nothing."), but in all the
nonverbal, gestural and body language with which we all
convey thoughts and feelings — in their squirming in their
seats, in their snickering and snorting, in their hands thrown
up in the air in gestures of impatience, in the way their eyes
met and exchanged "meaningful" glances, and in the way
the tension drained from their bodies when the exchange
was over.

Even small requests went unheeded. Early in 1970 both
teachers' organizations petitioned the board to declare Martin Luther King's birthday a school holiday. Every other
school district in the Bay Area, they claimed, memorialized
King's birthday. In order to ensure favorable action, the
teachers offered either to work an extra day to compensate
for the holiday, or to give up a holiday that was already
scheduled. Several people from the audience supported the
teachers' request, while USP spokesmen were articulate in
their objections. The board listened quietly throughout the
pleas and the discussion and finally left their audience
speechless when, *without a single word of response*, they
moved to the next item on the agenda.*

---

* Not a word of this exchange is recorded in the minutes of that
meeting, which is consonant with the conservative board's many attempts to make themselves look good on the record. Until the conservatives took office, the minutes were fairly full and faithful tran-

When I talked with the board members, I asked each why he had behaved thus and suggested that it might have relieved tensions in the district if they had granted the request. As if they had been programmed, the first response from each of them was some version of "I don't believe it's up to the school board to set national holidays." When I reminded them that the request was not for them to set a national holiday, but a school holiday, a typical reply was, "He wasn't a national figure. He was only important to a small percentage of the people, and I don't see why there ought to be a school holiday for him."

When I said that that "small percentage" of the people were currently feeling very deprived, they shrugged and said that it would make no difference what they did about King's birthday because "those people would find something else to complain about anyway." As for relieving black-white tensions in the district, one of them summed up their philosophy neatly:

> There's already too much emphasis put on race anyhow. People get sick and tired of being faced with race all the time. I know there are problems, but it doesn't help them any to keep forcing us to be involved with them all the time. Anyway, I don't believe in soft-soaping.

For the liberals and the blacks it would have been a gesture to "ease tensions"; for the white conservatives it would have been "soft-soaping." Not only the black-white problems,

---

scriptions of what had taken place at the meetings. Now they are carefully edited to present the picture of a calm, neutral, deliberative body at work. Moreover, whereas traditionally the tape recordings of school board meetings were available for public use, soon after the conservatives took office the board withdrew those tapes from public use and had them destroyed after transcription. Some liberals continued to pressure to hear the tapes before they were erased, and the board solved the problem permanently by announcing that board meetings would no longer be tape-recorded.

but the white-white problems will never be solved until we can somehow cross that boundary.

CENSORSHIP, CONFORMITY, AND FREEDOM

Since they came to power, the conservatives have kept up a steady pressure for conformity. Teachers hardly dare innovate any longer for fear of insults and reprisals. For example, early in 1970 a new course titled "Principles of Discussion" was presented to the board for adoption. The course was prepared in conformance with district regulations, and the proposal went through official channels, gaining the requisite approval at each step along the way. Thus, by the time it came before the board, the course had received the following impressive list of recommendations: at the school level, the members of the English Department where it would be taught and the instructional vice-principal and principal; at the district level, the chairmen of the English Departments of all the secondary schools, the secondary curriculum committee (composed of instructional vice-principals in the secondary schools), and the superintendent of schools and his cabinet. When the secondary school curriculum co-ordinator completed her presentation, the board sat quietly without exchanging a word. When they prepared to move to the next item on the agenda, *still wthout comment* on the proposal before them, a teacher asked why the board would not discuss the matter. The president replied that the board members "apparently feel that the course does not satisfy their requirements." "What must a teacher do to get a new course approved?" the speaker demanded. "Go through channels," the board president retorted coldly. Angry and shocked, the speaker responded, "Begging your indulgence, that is precisely what was done!" The president of the board, turning to the superintendent, "Next item on the agenda, please." The teachers sputtered helplessly.

One popular teacher — hardly a radical, but a man who is in tune with his students — said,

> I know that I'm constrained about what I can and cannot do, will or will not do these days. During the last two years teachers have been hesitant to do anything. You hear them say jokingly all the time, "Wonder what Fuller would think of *that*?" But while they seem to say it jokingly, they're very concerned. So most of them don't want to take any chances of stirring things up.

Many found that they "stirred things up" just by doing the things they had always done in their classrooms. One teacher who had made the *Freedom News* (a local radical monthly that is very antagonistic to the present school board) available to his students as part of a body of research materials was severely criticized. At first he was told that he must provide balance in his classroom, and if *Freedom News* was to be available, he must also make available *American Opinion* (the John Birch Society organ). Having no objections to exposing his students to all viewpoints, he agreed. Unsatisfied, the board members still objected; they did not care what else was presented, they said, but *Freedom News* would not be tolerated in any classroom in the RUSD. But the board never confronted the teacher directly. Instead, they kept the pressure on the downtown administration and the principal. The principal insistently "suggested" to the teacher that it was only "sensible" to placate the board. The superintendent was more blunt. "If I have to come down and deal with any more trouble from you, I'll fire you," he warned.

Other teachers, on orders from the board president, have been called to task by the administration for club projects such as an Ecology Club Clean-Up Day, which the board president interpreted as a demonstration that was disruptive to the educational process, a Black History Week display that included pictures of Black Panther leaders and Martin Luther King, and a dramatic presentation that the board decided (for unspecified reasons) might offend some sensibilities.

In an act that exposed them to widespread ridicule in the press and television, the board banned the use of the peace and the ecology symbols in the schools.* The president solemnly declared, "These so-called peace symbols are an insult to religious students because they are symbols of anti-Christ." An administration spokesman, trying to defend the action said,

> The use of symbols tends to divide society and what we are trying to do is accentuate the positive. The best example of this is President Nixon who is certainly leading us toward peace without the use of symbols, but with words and actions.

As a consequence of the repressive atmosphere, teachers censor themselves rather than waiting to hear "from downtown." For example, the board made plain its disapproval of the Vietnam Moratorium in the fall of 1969. As a result, while in districts all around the bay dozens of teachers were absent on that day, only five teachers remained away from their classrooms in the RUSD. Commenting on this, one teacher said, "that's because the board has instilled fear of their reactions so that only the really brave and courageous ones will dare to do anything like that."

Perhaps the silliest incident of self-censorship occurred when the principal of one of the elementary schools demanded that a third-grade teacher dispose of a little chicken hatchery that she was using to teach embryology because it violated the board's policy against sex education in the primary grades.

---

* The very next day a family sent their eight-year-old child to school bedecked with peace symbols from head to toe. When he was sent home from school, the parents protested to the American Civil Liberties Union which quickly won a court injunction against the ban.

Given the fact that they are protected by a lifetime tenure system, at first glance it seems strange that teachers should be so easily intimidated. But if one examines the structure of that system, it is no longer surprising. One of the primary facts about teacher tenure is that it is not transferable. If a teacher leaves a tenured job, he leaves the perquisites of tenure behind. To become tenured in another district requires three years' probationary service. In addition, promotion and salary increases are related to the number of years a teacher has served in the same district. Thus, once a teacher has taught in a district for twelve or thirteen years, he is at the top of the salary scale with lifetime security. To quit would mean to take a substantial salary cut and to accept an insecure probationary status elsewhere — an unlikely choice at any time, and even less likely now when school systems are suffering from severe budgetary crises and are cutting back their teaching staffs.

The security of the tenure system, coupled with promotional increments that are tied to the number of years in service, therefore, serve to lock a teacher in rather than to offer him freedom. At the same time, if he displeases his superiors, they have several weapons with which to make his life miserable even though they are unable to fire him. For example, they can transfer him against his will from school to school, giving him the least desirable assignments, or they can require him to teach subjects he hates. Knowing that he is bound into the system by virtue of the privileges he has accumulated, and at the same time knowing that his superiors can take punitive measures against him if he displeases them, the teacher is likely to acquiesce fairly readily even to repressive and unsatisfactory teaching conditions.

The teachers' bind gives the administration and school board an enormous advantage over them. Indeed, it substantially defuses the most powerful weapon a teachers union has—the strike. For the administration always has the sure knowledge that, even if the teachers lose the strike, most will be back in their classrooms rather than rushing off to take jobs in the district next door. The more experienced the teacher, the more years he has in service, the more likely that is to be true.

Besides these pressures for conformity on teachers and students and the subtle censorship that is implied in them, more overt forms of censorship are common throughout the system. The libraries and classrooms, for example, are being stripped of books that offend either the very restrictive morals or the politics of the conservatives. Often it is like shadowboxing to find out what happened and why. Everyone has a different story; no one ever seems to know quite how or why a book happens to have disappeared.

One such case concerned *The Learning Tree*, a novel by the well-known black author and photographer Gordon Parks, which deals with the inner lives of a black family struggling to learn to accept and to live in a hostile white world. In the spring of 1970, English teachers in Richmond High School who were using the book in their classrooms were ordered to turn in all copies. The books were, I was told, "put away somewhere," and efforts by teachers to get them back were unavailing. As some teachers protested and called upon administrators to explain their action, the situation became more and more mystifying. Administrators in both the school and in district headquarters said they did not know who initiated the complaint about the book or who gave the order to withdraw it from the classrooms.

The principal of Richmond High originally said that he was told by an official from central administrative headquarters to withdraw the book because a member of the school board had given that order. Since such intervention by a board member violates district policy for handling complaints about books, some teachers instituted grievance procedures. The official in question from district headquarters said that no board member had given such an order and that the school's principal had been mistaken. The action, he said, has been taken on the initiative of the superintendent (a procedure consonant with district policy). While he could not recall the superintendent's specific objections to the book, he thought he had judged it to be obscene and profane.

Educational television, too, was attacked sharply. Always leery of classroom television, for the first year the conservative board censored certain programs they found offensive or too liberal. During their first discussion of educational television in 1969, some board members said that they had no objections to the "academic" programs that taught science and mathematics, but those dealing with such matters as the Bill of Rights, freedom of speech, and the like were to them "liberal propaganda that has nothing to do with academics." [2] When one of the administrators objected that such programs properly fall into the category of social studies and that the Bill of Rights would seem to him to be "a major historical document," * one board member shouted, "What will they teach kids in such a program? To go out and demonstrate in the streets?" [3] †

In the fall of 1970, the administration came before the board with a recommendation to renew the annual contract with KQED, the award-winning local educational television station. By that time, the majority of the board members knew they would not vote for it. In fact, more than two months earlier a USP leader had told me,

> You can be sure we won't have KQED again next year. We took Jim Shattuck apart for his vote last year and he won't

---

* At that time, the profeessionals in the administration still dared to risk an occasional independent opinion, but no longer does one hear any.

† Again, this exchange does not appear in the minutes.

do that again. We got both Jim and Virgil [Gay], and they'll
have plenty to answer if anything goes wrong this time.

Wishing to override its administration's recommendation,
but unwilling to provoke a head-on controversy over the
matter, the board simply voted to table it. A storm of protest followed, and the matter was reopened two months
later, at which time they charged KQED programing with
"liberal political bias" and rejected the contract on a 3-2
vote, the two opposing votes coming from one board member who has retained some independence from the group
pressure and from another who is an upper-middle-class attorney.* Epitomizing the quality of the conservative discussion was this impassioned statement from the USP president.

> Parents are entitled to more than highly paid teachers as
> babysitters for KQED . . . Teachers now are paid between
> $8 and $16 per hour, and if they need outside help perhaps
> the district should look at the quality of the teachers it em-
> ploys . . . It is time that this board stop subsidizing radical
> liberal establishments such as KQED which represents every-
> thing the board is against. KQED must go!

To this a representative of a teachers' organization responded, "These types of statements are responsible for
teacher militancy." And the board president (in an angry
reply that was also deleted from the minutes) retorted,
"Maybe they're a *response to* teacher militancy."

* The outcry against taking television out of the schools was
much greater than the conservatives had expected; many of their
own supporters were ired. Consequently, the board negotiated a
contract with a smaller local station which can be received only
on sets equipped with UHF receivers and which broadcasts fourteen
of KQED's twenty-eight programs. In twenty-seven elementary schools
the district had to install UHF antennae before they could receive
the new channel; in seventeen more, reception was only possible
through cable television — a high price this economy-minded board
paid to punish KQED.

While for many people the removal of KQED from the schools seemed a serious impairment of the breadth and quality of education, the conservative board's action was not without some rationality from their perspective. First, KQED does have a liberal orientation, and it presents rather sophisticated and cosmopolitan programing. Second, its news department had been less than kind to the conservative officials of the district. Third, this was the station that was responsible for the distribution of "Time of Your Life," a sex education film series that the conservatives despised. So deep did feelings against the station run, that several conservative parents told me that they did not permit their children to watch it because "the programs are too liberal" and because they often show "those Berkeley hippies as if they approve of people who look and act like that."

In addition, before the conservatives took over the direction of the schools, they were in a state of rage because they believed that their children were being exposed to alien values and life styles in the classroom, and they feared that this exposure would eventually separate them from parents and home. Since, as they saw it, KQED educational television was a major promulgator of those alien values, it was quite logical that they should ban it from the schools. The USP president was quite right when he said that KQED "represents everything the board is against."

THE NEW BOARD AND THE OLD: A COMPARISON

While the former liberal board had been less than totally responsive to conservative demands, it had made attempts — some serious, some pretenses — to compromise and conciliate. The conservatives, however, generally have not even bothered to go through the motions. It remains to speculate about the reasons for those vivid differences between the two boards. I have already indicated that the differences in social characteristics are at least partly responsible for their differing political attitudes and behavior. In addition, I would suggest two other factors: their different political affiliations and participation histories, and their disparate views of the relationship of an elected official to a constituency — perspectives rooted in their disparate political philosophies.

POLITICAL AFFILIATION AND PARTICIPATION HISTORY

In the domain of political affiliations, the ousted liberal board members were split, with three of their number claiming registration in the Republican party and three claiming to be Democrats. Of the conservatives, on the other hand, four are Republicans and one a Democrat. Political party affiliation, however, is no longer a very informative variable, nor is it necessarily a predictor of voting behavior. In the 1968 presidential election, the conservative Democrat voted for George Wallace, while none of the three liberal Republicans voted for Richard Nixon.*

Despite the fact that all of these men and women had been (or were then) elected officials in the community, all but one described themselves as not politically active.† In part, this stems from the belief that schools are nonpolitical institutions — a belief that is part of a larger American myth which holds that by labeling an activity nonpartisan, it thereby becomes nonpolitical. This notion leads people to

* These voting patterns held throughout the study. Among fifteen conservatives interviewed, three voted for Wallace in 1968. One of the three was registered to the American Independent party; the other two were Democrats. Of the five registered Democrats on the conservative side, two voted for Wallace, two for Nixon, and one for Humphrey. One volunteered that he had voted for Goldwater in 1964. On the liberal side, of sixteen respondents, five were registered Republicans, but all voted for Humphrey.

† Among the entire sample of thirty-one lay leaders and board members, only five liberals and six conservatives characterized themselves as politically active.

perceive a curious disjunction between community and political participation and between nonpartisan and partisan political activity. Thus, two liberals who served on the boards of a half-dozen or more city, county, and state agencies, including the school board, said, "I've never done anything of consequence politically." Another liberal who had served as mayor of one of the cities in the district said, "I've never been active politically."

When I asked for digests of their participation in community activities and organizations, two of the liberals and four of the conservatives replied that they were not involved in community activities and that they "never belonged to anything." The common cry was, "We're not joiners." "My wife says I've always been a loner." "I'm a hermit." But when I probed beyond that initial response, the liberals who had given that reply remembered that they had served on the boards of such community agencies as the Richmond Model Cities program, the Richmond Planning Commission, and North Richmond Neighborhood House. In fact, the histories of participation of the liberals were rich, revealing high rates of activity and a wide range of interests. Not only did they participate in organizations in their own neighborhoods, but in city, county, and state organizations and agencies representing a variety of interests. In addition, four of the six liberal board members had previously exhibited some concern for the problems of the black community and were members of the board of the North Richmond Neighborhood House, an organization concerned with the troubled youth of North Richmond's black ghetto.

On the conservative side, however, no matter how I rephrased the question, prompted, or prodded, the answers remained essentially the same: participation histories were almost barren. One board member said he belonged to two men's service clubs and two fraternal organizations. One remembered that several years before, he had served on the community council of his neighborhood; and the other three said they were concerned only with school affairs. Interestingly enough, however, only one was actively involved in school matters before the busing controversy arose. That these men had not been visible in the larger political community before the school crisis may explain, in part, their lack of responsiveness to any but their own adherents. Since they came to prominence within the framework of a special-purpose organization, they faced few or none of the constraints of maintaining a previous community position. Since they belonged to few, if any, other organizations, they felt none of the cross-pressures that derive from multiple group affiliation. Finally, since they came into public life at a time when the district was profoundly polarized, their continued isolation from those of different persuasions was ensured. Except for the public exchanges, which too often turned out to be hostile shouting matches, members of the opposing forces almost never met on a person-to-person basis.

The Board Members and the Community

Together, these differences led also to differences in the ways the liberals and conservatives viewed their role as board members vis-à-vis the community. In general, the liberals insisted that they were not committed to a particular constituency or segment of the community, but felt responsible to the entire district. And, indeed, their many attempts to compromise with the conservatives in order to palliate their discontent give substance to this claim. Their behavior over the issue of sex education is illustrative.

Contrary to the liberal belief, the conservative view generally is that sex education is a function of the home, not the school. Even those who agree that some kind of sex education in school is desirable balk at "anything that deals with people or emotions." One conservative respondent summarized that position well:

> Personally, I think you can teach reproduction in a biological way without emphasis on sex. That's what I object to, the emphasis on sex and the whole emotional part.

Acting on those beliefs, the district's conservatives organized a movement to ban the showing of the sex-education film series "The Time of Your Life." After several months of dissension, the liberal board finally compromised and agreed that the films would no longer be shown during class. Instead, they stipulated that the films could be shown only before or after school or during the lunch hour, and only with written parental consent.

To the liberal board, this was a reasonable compromise. And while some of their liberal constituency might have wished it could be otherwise, they accepted the compromise as one of the cost of governing in a heterogeneous society. Now no child would see the film series without parental consent, nor would any child be deprived of class time while others viewed it. At the same time, this kind of education would be available to those children whose parents wished them to have it. Since the district already owned the films, there was no cost involved, and no one could complain legitimately that public funds were being spent for frills or immoral purposes.

The conservatives, however, saw it another way. Once in power, they, who had insisted that only they, as parents, had a right to determine what their children would or would not be permitted to see or to read, did not hesitate to dictate to others. Hence, four months after they were seated, the conservative board voted to discontinue the "Time of Your Life" series. To ensure that no future board could easily reverse their decision, the video tapes were either given away or destroyed. (Both alternatives were under serious consideration, but no conclusion was reached in public session.) The pleas of the liberals that this would deprive their children of what they considered a valuable educational experience went unheard.

Since their own children were safe from exposure to these films, why would the conservative board not permit them to be shown for those who wanted to see them? The answer is probably two-fold. First, they saw the whole matter as a moral question and believed that it was dangerously immoral for any child to be exposed to the films. Second, three of the five men said that they believed it was their duty to represent the people who elected them, and those people wanted the films thrown out of the schools. Said one,

> . . . a board member has the responsibility of keeping faith with all those who elected him . . . I don't look upon public office as being elected to *think* for the people but to *represent* them, to vote in their stead since they can't all be there voting for themselves.

Referring to another issue on which he voted against the wishes of his constituency, another conservative board member said,

> I won't do that again. I voted wrong. I entered this facet of my life feeling that I was not going to follow in the footsteps of every other politician I know of. We elect a congressman, for example, to represent us in Washington, and within six months he's representing Washington to the people. . . . Maybe I wasn't even wrong on the issue, but the people I represent don't see it that way, and that's what counts. I view my role *strictly* as one of representing my constituency.

I asked, "What about the other people who hold another point of view? Who represents them?" He replied,

> I learned early that you don't satisfy all the people. My idea of representative government is not that I'm so smart that I would know all the answers, or even that my constituency is so smart that they'll know it all. But if I can vote the way

they want me to, if I can vote as they would if they were voting for themselves, then I'm doing my job.

Their constricted and localized history of community participation made that perspective possible, it left them relatively free to meet the expectations of their constituency.

Two of the conservative board members belonged to USP; one served on its executive board. The only one of the five who has remained relatively independent of the organization is viewed by its leaders with suspicion.

A high officer in USP told me that he considered the role of the organization to be that of "a watchdog of the board to make sure they do their job right." When they do not, he said, "We take them apart, and they know we're not foolin' around." And, indeed, they were not "foolin' around." Within a few months after the conservatives took office, the president of USP, angered by the board's position on a routine matter of expenditures, publicly chastised and threatened them.

> The people of this district have just finished dumping a board because they had refused to give the public access to information. I hope that we won't have to face this problem again with this board, but please remember that what happened to the last board could happen again.[4]

The board beat a hasty retreat.

What difference, one may ask, was there between USP's relationship to the conservative board and CEE's with their liberal predecessors? The former board did, after all, have close personal and social ties with people in CEE leadership. And certainly CEE leaders coaxed, cajoled, threatened, and bullied the liberal board to adopt positions that were compatible with theirs. Sometimes they succeed, but unlike the situation between USP and the conservative board, sometimes they did not. And often CEE leaders compromised their demands (witness the sex education issue) as they sought to help the board respond to the demands of the conservative community.

The difference is due not to different kinds of relationships between the boards and the organizations in question, but to the different political philosophies to which the groups adhered. For the liberals, moral issues gave way to political reality and to the belief that politics in America is the art of compromise; the conflict of competing groups must be kept within reasonable bounds. Thus, the liberal board expressed deep concern over the polarization of the community and sought desperately, if futilely, for ways to bridge the chasm. The liberal sector of their constituency, while sometimes impatient, sometimes ambivalent, sometimes angry, and always suffering from internal disunity, largely shared that concern and understood the board members' efforts to palliate the conflict.

For the conservatives, on the other hand, the majority not only rules, it dominates; and the obligation of society's minorities is to submit. That may seem an anomalous statement since the conservatives did not submit when they were in a minority position. The point, however, is that they always believed that they were an actual majority regardless of the outcome of electoral politics, and it is that majority of which they spoke when they argued that majority rules. The need to safeguard minorities from what Tocqueville called the tyranny of the majority was an alien notion. This philosophy was expressed quite clearly by the conservative board president:

> We're saying that our philosophy prevailed and we're just carrying out the mandate given to us by the people who elected us. They're the majority, and majority rules.

Finally, the liberals tended to be aware that they could be wrong; hence, they avoided absolutes. For the conservatives, however, their conviction about the rightness of their position and the righteousness of their cause was so profound as to be unshakable. As a leading conservative political scientist explains, for them there are no open questions; they "couldn't care less if they get caught assuming their own infallibility."[5]

In sum, consonant with their clearly articulated commitment to the will of their limited conservative constituency, and probably reinforced by their constricted experiences in the political world, almost no attempt was made to hide their anger and contempt for the liberals and blacks; and few efforts were visible to compromise any issues. Since it is not possible to tap their constituency's "will" very readily, it means, in fact, that they have been bound to the will of USP. Since that organization has been functioning at a minimal level since 1969, in reality it reduces itself to the fact that a handful of active USP leaders have dictated policy. For the board members, who are in almost complete accord with these articulate people, there is no conflict. How well this does, indeed, represent the will of the more than 30,000 people who voted for them is an open question.

The repressive atmosphere in the district is taking its toll, not so much in identifiable and dramatic events, but quietly and insidiously. Thoughtful teachers have become ever more fearful. There is safety in erring on the side of caution; consequently, programs have been constrained and constricted, and new courses or new material for existing courses have been proposed less often.

Meanwhile, the liberals who retreated in disarray have remained in that state. Convinced that they could not win through the political process, they turned to the courts. But there has been little vindication of their hopes as the district has bargained for and won a series of delays that have already bought it more than two years' worth of time and the possibility of a changed political climate in the courts.

For the present, then, the dream of desegregating the ghetto schools is dead, and the conservatives have met with important successes in their attempts to restructure the RUSD schools into a system more compatible with their political and educational philosophies. How stable their hegemony over the district will be, is yet to be seen. Two board seats came up for election again in 1971 and although the incumbents won reelection, enthusiasm was lacking, voter turnout dropped by more than 54 percent, and their margin of victory was significantly smaller than in 1969.*

* In 1969 48,469 people cast their votes; 22,136 did in 1971. The margin of victory in 1969 was 2½–1; in 1971 it dropped to 1½–1.

PART FIVE

RACE, CLASS, AND DEMOCRACY

CHAPTER **11** **CONCLUSION**

This, then, has been the story of the mobilization and polarization of a community around a struggle to desegregate its schools. To the question, what accounted for the success of the mobilization against busing, the most obvious answer is racism. On every dimension of racism — stereotyping, hostility, unreasoning fear, sexual fantasies, prejudice, and discrimination — the working-class and lower-middle-class conservatives were more overtly racist and less guilty about it than the upper-middle-class liberals. This, of course, should come as no surprise given the well-documented observation that there is an inverse correlation between education and prejudice; that is, the lower the level of education, the higher the level of prejudice.[1]

But I started this study with the assumption that America is a racist society and that the most overt expression of that racism is to be found among working-class and lower-middle-class people. It was not my intention to spend more than two years to document the obvious. Therefore, I sought other answers to the two questions that dominated this research: What were the weaknesses in the moderate-liberal coalition that resulted in its failure to integrate the Richmond schools and in its subsequent ouster from power? What were the strengths among the conservatives that enabled them to mobilize what had been a relatively apathetic constituency to reverse integration plans and to implement their own educational philosophy? The answers to both questions are to be found in the social-structural realities that dominated the lives of the people involved. The liberal failure is not the failure of the men and women who were the central actors; rather, it is the failure of liberal politics — a case history of its inability to cope with an issue that arouses strong feelings, that divides the society deeply, and that brings large numbers of formerly inactive men and women into the political arena. Similarly, the conservative success is rooted in a sociopolitical system that has too often failed to hear, to understand, and to react to the needs of those in the working class and lower-middle class. It is the price we pay for what has been an essentially elitist and undemocratic society.

The liberal school board members were plagued by two dilemmas that prevented their establishing clear and unequivocal goals. First, they were beset by the same ambivalence about integration that troubles much of liberal America.* Publicly they insisted that integrated schools

* A television news broadcast in December 1971 revealed that, with only one exception, every Democratic presidential aspirant (announced and unannounced) and most liberal congressmen, senators, and journalists in Washington, D.C., sent their children to private schools. One nationally syndicated columnist, an articulate critic of those who oppose school integration, said ruefully: "Nobody wants to make their children pay for their own social philosophy." The wife of a liberal congressman said, just like one of the respondents in this study, "Your children only get educated once."

would benefit all children, and repeated it over and over as if reciting a litany. Privately, and for some perhaps unconsciously, they shared the prejudices and stereotypes of those who were most racially antagonistic. They were never certain that black children were not really intellectually inferior to their own and that their presence in the classroom would not downgrade the quality of education. As they tried to act on both sides of that ambivalence, they were, of course, unable to act on either. Martin Meyerson and Edward Banfield noted the same internal conflict in a controversy over the selection of sites for public housing in Chicago.

> The struggle over site selection was not altogether a struggle among opposing interests or groups; in part *it was a struggle among conflicting tendencies within the same interest.* . . . On the one hand, the leaders of the Council wanted some public housing. On the other hand, they did not want to do anything that would encourage the spread of Negroes into the outlying white neighborhoods.[2] [*Emphasis added.*]

The ambivalence of the liberal board members in Richmond resulted in an ambiguity of goals that hindered action for several years. When, under threat of court action they were finally forced to act, their plans were incoherent, inept, and politically unfair — incoherent and inept, perhaps because their internal conflicts left them with a less than conscious wish to fail; unfair, because they offered educational inducements to their professional upper-middle-class constituency but not to the rest of the community. In part the payoff to the upper-middle-class liberals was the result of a political calculation that this was the way to seduce them into accepting a busing plan; but — and this may be more important — it was also due to the assumptions of both the liberal school board members and their friends that it was in the natural order of things that those bright, upper-middle-class children would be provided with the best educational

facilities the district could offer. I do not suggest that anyone deliberately conspired to present these already well-
favored children with a better educational break than the
others. There was no need for that. For the school board
members and most of their white supporters shared the same
upper-middle-class background, life style, beliefs, attitudes,
and values, and, as with all people, their behavior flowed
almost automatically from those facts of their lives. With
just two exceptions, none of the integrationist respondents
in this study saw anything amiss in the fact that their children would be sent to the new and extraordinarily advan-
taged Martin Luther King School. They accepted that as
natural. These were, after all, the highest achieving children
in the district — as several of them said, "the cream of the
crop" — the group from which would come tomorrow's
leaders. Once that definition was accepted, as it was almost universally, was it not the duty of society's leaders to
protect and nourish such assets?

Second, and not unrelated, the liberal school board
members suffered from a conflict between their coexistent
beliefs in popular democracy and in an elite meritocracy,
political concepts that impress inconsistent and incongruent
demands upon the political actors holding them. They
shared — or at least wished to believe in — the ideal of
classical democratic theory that not only the individual but
the democracy itself would benefit if popular participation
and understanding were raised. But simultaneously they dis-
trusted mass participation and wished to circumscribe it
carefully, for they feared that to invite large-scale participation in policy-making would be fatal to democracy. On the
more positive level, however, they were also convinced that
an educated elite would bring some special expertise to
the art of governing, that by virtue of its higher status and
higher educational level, such an elite was able to transcend
self-interest for the well-being of the community.

Caught in this dilemma, the liberals were hesitant to use their power to mandate integration, while, at the same time, they were fearful of the consequences of inviting serious public discussion. Thus, they resorted to the traditional rituals of governments that claim to be representative and cloaked their attempts to legitimate their behavior in the *forms* of democratic participation. They appointed a lay study commission and held a series of public discussions. But it was form without substance, for those acts had little relation to the formation of public policy. Instead, they were the operations of the performing government. The decisions had long since been taken by the actual government; the remaining problem was how to clothe them in the kind of legitimacy the liberals needed to enable them to act. But strong feelings about school integration had brought unusually large numbers of people into the political arena, and those devices only served to anger the newcomers who charged that the commissions and meetings were a sham designed to keep them from participating in the decision-making process. *Once an issue becomes salient to a significant sector of the public, the mechanisms with which political leaders generally palliate conflict and soothe discontent fail to work.*

Given the contradictions in the political philosophy of the liberal school board members and their ambivalence about the impact of school desegregation on educational quality, they were immobilized whenever the opposition raised its voice. That indecisiveness played a central part in facilitating the mobilization of the anti-integrationists, for any challenge to customary ways typically arouses anxiety which, if not relieved, arouses resistance. The appointment of the Committee on De Facto Segregation constituted such a challenge, and the years of irresolution heightened the anxieties. The resistance that is aroused can be relieved in one of two ways: either by returning to the *status quo ante* or by implementing the change quickly so that the living reality is substituted for the vague apprehensions. If the latter course is adopted, the energy used to defend against the anxiety and all the fantasies it provokes probably will be released and diverted to deal with the concrete problems that attend any social change.

There is some evidence to support these speculations. Writing not long after the 1954 *Brown* v. *Board of Education* decision, Gordon Allport noted:

> Experience shows that most citizens accept a forthright *fait accompli* with little protest or disorder. In part they do so because integrationist policies are usually in line with their own consciences (even though countering their prejudices). *In part the swift change is accepted because opposing forces have no time to mobilize and launch a counter-movement.* [Therefore] it probably would have been psychologically sounder for the Supreme Court to have insisted upon prompt acquiescence with its ruling of 1954. "Deliberate speed" does not fix an early and inescapable date for compliance.[3] [*Emphasis added.*]

The history of the intervening years has validated that judgment. Even now it is not too late for decisive action by legitimate authorities to forestall the mobilization of an anti-integrationist opposition. In his study of the successful desegregation of the schools in Teaneck, New Jersey, Reginald Damerell argued persuasively that the outcome would have been different if the community had not been faced with a *fait accompli*:

> The victory, it is important to remember, was for an integration plan *in operation.* Had the sixth-grade plan not been in effect but only *proposed* for the coming year, chances are that Kaplan, Sampson, and Foah would have won as Warner and Margolis had the year before . . . . *Integration, in other words, presents something of a paradox: It is an idea most*

whites fear and dread and resist hysterically, yet accept when it happens. Courage and leadership are necessary to make it happen.[4] [*Emphasis added.*]

Moreover, in the fall of 1970 when such southern cities as Charlotte, North Carolina, and Richmond, Roanoke, and Lynchburg, Virginia, complied with federal court orders to integrate their schools by instituting massive busing plans, neither the threatened boycotts nor the violent protests materialized. The Charlotte-Mecklenburg district, it is true, went to the Supreme Court to seek relief from the order of a federal district judge. But while awaiting that decision, school officials moved resolutely toward getting the children settled in their new schools. In all four districts, most parents complied peacefully when it became clear that there was no acceptable alternative.

The city of San Francisco also suffered months of turmoil and violence early in 1970 when its school board was discussing the experimental integration of a complex of twelve elementary schools in a plan that called for busing. Yet when school opened in September, the children lined up peacefully to wait for their buses, and their parents seemed to have accepted the inevitable. In fact, some two months later, when a few parents attempted to build a protest, they could never muster more than twenty-five families in support (out of more than two thousand children involved), and that number dwindled quickly as the failure became clear. The following year, 1971, with a city-wide busing plan in the offing, the tumult grew louder, and opponents threatened, among other things, to bankrupt the district with a massive boycott. On the first day of school in September, more than 40 percent of the city's 41,000 elementary school children stayed home. Within a week, as parents began to perceive that the business of educating the young in the San Francisco schools would proceed with or without their children, and as they felt reassured that children who climbed aboard a bus in the morning did, indeed, return whole and happy in the afternoon, the boycott began to crumble. Two months later, only about 4,000 children (less than 10 percent of the city's elementary school population) were still not enrolled in the public schools, and district officials reported a continuing steady rate of return.* Of those still boycotting, at least 1,500 are residents of Chinatown, where resistance to busing was especially acute because many Chinese elders feared that taking the children out of the neighborhood would destroy what remained of the old culture. Even so, more than 5,000 Chinese children remained in the public schools.

Finally, the school superintendent in Seattle, Washington, commenting on unsuccessful attempts to desegregate that city's schools, argued recently that public hearings arranged by "timid" public officials only aggravated tensions.

> I underestimated the virulence of white racism. . . . We should have done the whole business back in 1966, prior to some of the frustrations and anger that have developed over the years. . . . Voluntary transfers . . . and other piecemeal steps only produced divisiveness in the community.[5]

Looking back over the years of the RUSD struggle, it seems probable that the school board could have implemented integration successfully at any time from the birth of the district in 1965 to the fall of 1968. But they were never able to act decisively during that time, and their in-

---

* Critics of the integration program in San Francisco point to what they call the exodus from the city of families who will neither put their children in private schools nor on buses. In a city where mobility is high (12,000 students left the city during the 1970/1971 school year whereas 10,500 moved into the city), *during the first three months of the 1971/1972 school year, only 2,000 elementary school children moved out of the city.* Comparing the two years, the 1971/1972 rate seems more like a trickle than an exodus.

decision encouraged the opposition and facilitated its mobilization. By the time they did take the step, it was too late, for their plans called for implementation in the fall of 1969 while they faced an election in the spring of that year that promised almost certain defeat.

These, then, were the crucial weaknesses of the liberals, but what was the basis of the conservatives' strength? That is harder to assess, perhaps because the very alien nature of the movement and its participants make it more difficult for an upper-middle-class social scientist to understand. Traditionally, liberal social scientists have explained such mass movements with concepts such as status politics or the authoritarian predisposition of their adherents. They have argued that we must guard against these movements because they are invariably authoritarian or totalitarian in nature. Only a society made up of competing, special interest pressure groups will ensure democracy, they have insisted.

These are tempting answers. They do not challenge our role in the social system; they do not call upon us to examine critically the existing order which deals with us so comfortably; they place the responsibility for the dissent on some inadequacy of the dissidents. But as Michael Rogin comments, "It is a mistake to identify mass movements with authoritarianism and pressure groups with democracy. Rather there are authoritarian and democratic mass movements, just as there are authoritarian and democratic pressure groups." [6]

In rejecting these traditional notions, I have pointed out that the working-class and lower-middle-class whites who dominated the movement to oppose integration are the people most immediately threatened by any upward mobility among blacks. For them, race was never an abstract problem far from home (as it was for so many of the upper-middle-class liberals), for it is to their jobs, their neighborhoods, their schools that the first challenge is made. With little to show for a lifetime of hard work and striving, they are not apt to be persuaded to make room for newcomers — black or white. We see here the operation of what Melvin Tumin calls the "principle of the *most proximate pecker*," which says, "The most serious status clashes occur between the newly arisen group and those closest to them in the status-pecking order."[7]

Thus, it would seem that the major strength of the conservative drive probably lay in the fact that for too long the definition of the public good had been made by a small, relatively self-contained elite — a definition that too frequently accorded with their own self-interest and largely left the working class and lower-middle class out. With the movement to integrate the schools, the latter group felt desperately threatened, for despite the overwhelming evidence in the RUSD and elsewhere that the school system has helped to rigidify and solidify the caste and class systems of the nation, that it does not serve either black or white working class children equally or adequately,[8] most people continue to believe that the schools are the singular agency of upward mobility in the society. And despite reassurances to the contrary, the racist ethos of America predisposes most people to believe that black children in a classroom downgrade the quality of education there.

Feeling powerless and deeply threatened, and therefore passionately angry, the working-class and lower-middle-class anti-integrationists moved into the political arena in large numbers. Fearful that they would bear the lion's share of the costs of the impending social change — a fear that was intensified by an integration plan in Richmond that offered them no visible benefits — they reached for the stereotypes that reinforced their prejudices and that legitimated the scapegoating of blacks. But it ill befits the upper-middle-class professionals to look upon that behavior disdainfully.

For, tragically, now that significant numbers of minorities are knocking at the university door — that formerly sacred, all-white preserve — we keep hearing the academicians and the professionals cry, "We can't lower academic standards. Would you want a less than qualified doctor to take care of you?" *That cry, however, ignores the fact that for many of the poor and minorities of the nation the question is not the *qualifications* of a doctor, but *whether there is one at all*. It is a cry, moreover, that sounds very little different to my ear than that of the carpenter who stoutly maintained in a recent television broadcast, "I'm not prejudiced, but we can't have guys who don't know anything about construction on the job. Would you want to live in a house built by guys who don't know where to put the nails and the beams?"

The thrust of my argument here is that America's so-called silent majority has been left out of the political process far too long and that, in part, their present anger is a response to that political fact. The implication is that unless we find ways to ensure large-scale popular participation by all sectors of the community, we can look forward to such political upheavals whenever the issues stir any significant portion of the populace. Yet I have also suggested that the liberal school board members could have exercised the power that was theirs, and, despite public resistance mandated a fair integration program, one that met some of the real educational needs of working-class and lower-middle-class children. Are those two arguments inconsistent? I believe not.

I hold strongly to the notions embodied in classical

---

* Or, if the reader prefers, we can substitute for medicine any other discipline in the academy. To take the one I know best, sociology, the question might be paraphrased, "Would you want a less than qualified sociologist to write books about you?" The answer by both working-class whites and blacks is, bitterly, "That's what we already have."

democratic theory that both the democracy and the public interest are intimately related to the growth and development of the citizens of the community and inseparable from the vitality of their participation in the political process. I believe in the promise of classical theory that democracy ought to be an agency of self-development, and that people must assume responsibility for their lives and for the institutions within which they live in order to develop an active, critical posture toward their environment — a necessary ingredient for intelligent participation in the democratic process. Thus, I will argue that we must find our way toward a democracy in which political and personal lives are enriched by popular participation. But the belief that such a democracy is possible is predicated upon major changes in the structure of our political institutions. Meanwhile, there are decisions to be made, grievances to be redressed, injustices to be set right — none possible in our present society without strong and courageous leaders. In the RUSD desegregation struggle, the question was and is: Given the existing sociopolitical system, what were the rights and responsibilities of leadership?

To argue that the liberal leaders had a primary responsibility to educate their constituency regarding the desirability of integrating the schools is sophistic, since it fails to take account of the context in which such education would be undertaken and which would practically dictate its failure. A working class and lower-middle class, trapped by the values of the system into a frenetic chase for goods and security and never quite making it, are unlikely to risk what little they have by allowing blacks to move up. Indeed, a citizenry mired in such a socioeconomic bind, riddled with racial fears and hostilities, and unskilled and untutored in political participation is not likely to be readily educated in the fundamentals of democracy. Once activated, they rely, instead, on a vulgar and rigid majoritarianism to support their undemocratic politics and refuse to acknowledge the rights of minorities. This is, in part, a response to their belief that for too long they (the majority) have been ruled by an upper-middle-class minority. Is this belief an irrational projection or fantasy, or a realistic assessment of the political reality of democratic politics in America today? I suggest the latter, for this is a political system in which most people are neither educated for nor encouraged in political participation. In fact, on the average, 40 percent of the population does not even participate in presidential elections, and nonvoters come disproportionately from the lower classes — political facts that are applauded by some of the most prominent social theorists of our time who insist that the health of the system depends upon that apathy.

Under those conditions, the liberal school board's attempt to persuade its opposition before taking action was, in fact, to sanction more unconscionable delays in redressing the legitimate grievances of black parents and their children. And the liberals were quite well aware of that. Indeed, that is precisely the reason that several board members gave for not appointing a politically balanced study commission. It would mean, they said, that integration proposals would be talked to death. Yet, despite that awareness, they equivocated. The reasons, as always, are complex, and I have discussed some in detail. One more might be added here: the Richmond black community, while clearly favoring integration, showed no immediate signs of the kind of militancy that elsewhere had forced white decision-makers to move in fear. Thus, throughout the years of the struggle, the liberals were free to reason that it was not their fault that they were stymied; they wished it could be otherwise, but their commitment to the democratic process prevented action. They had no choice, they said, but to heed the claims of their white opponents. That reasoning, however, only serves to disguise the fact that inaction is also a political choice that carries with it social consequences. In fact, they chose to defer the rights of blacks to the demands of whites. As John Sharnik has eloquently pointed out, when faced with the need to respond to political demands, white decision-makers interpret the requirements of democracy quite differently depending upon the color of the "demanders."[9]

Indeed, to insist that the rules of democracy required that the school board be bound by the will of the majority was to deny the oppressive and undemocratic consequences to blacks of that white majority will. More important, it was to fail to grasp that one of the most vexing political problems of late-twentieth-century America is not how to ensure majority rule, but how to protect minorities from majority tyranny.[10]

Finally, to those critics who insist that they oppose busing because it wastes valuable time and does not touch upon fundamental educational problems, I commend the words of Senator Philip Hart of Michigan:

> Yes, busing may be inconvenient, but how much more "inconvenient" will it be for our children tomorrow if we do not move to heal the split which threatens the nation today? Undoubtedly, a child does not learn arithmetic while riding a bus and busing alone will not insure a quality education, but life will not be very good for the best mathematician if indeed the country is at war within itself when he or she becomes an adult.

APPENDIX

APPENDIX

APPENDIX

Table A1. Socioeconomic Status (SES) and
Median Reading Scores of Elementary
Schools in the RUSD, 1968

School	SES	Percent Black	Median Reading Scores		
			Grade 1	Grade 3	Grade 6
Kensington	2.0	1%	94%	92%	86%
Madera	2.2	19	65	88	75
El Monte	2.8	19	94	77	81
Del Mar	3.0	7	87	77	64
Valley View	3.4	0	89	77	63
Ellerhorst	3.6	0	60	57	69
Fairmede	3.6	10	49	48	54
Harding	3.6	4	72	75	67
Olinda	3.6	0	49	59	48
Castro	3.8	2	81	71	71
Fairmont	3.8	0	51	65	50
Grant	3.8	19	79	47	37
Mira Vista	3.8	8	76	75	67
Collins	4.3	0	71	59	56
Stewart	4.3	0	32	45	40
Tara Hills	4.3	0	68	57	54
Sheldon	4.4	9	76	69	60
Ford	4.6	19	58	47	50
Kerry Hills	4.6	0	55	55	51
Coronado	4.7	98	30	25	24
Serra	4.7	3	72	55	66
Washington	4.7	37	37	47	37
Alvarado	4.8	17	72	55	62
Balboa	4.8	19	55	69	50
Murphy	4.8	10	65	57	50

Table A1 (continued) Socioeconomic Status (SES) and Median Reading Scores of Elementary Schools in the RUSD, 1968

School	SES	Percent Black	Median Reading Scores		
			Grade 1	Grade 3	Grade 6
Wilson	4.8	9	81	48	60
Bayview	4.9	19	49	45	32
Hillview	5.0	1	47	55	50
Riverside	5.0	8	47	47	38
Montalvin Manor	5.1	0	51	37	47
Rancho	5.1	0	45	50	28
Shannon	—	—	45	59	47
King	5.2	94	22	37	24
Stege	5.2	74	47	45	32
El Portal	5.3	7	42	54	38
Belding	5.4	6	51	52	47
Broadway	5.5	0	45	61	42
Lincoln	5.7	47	47	18	17
Cortez	5.8	85	60	23	17
Dover	5.8	2	32	36	37
Lake	5.8	37	51	21	19
Nystrom	5.9	93	35	28	14
Peres	6.0	91	45	12	16
Verde	6.0	97	22	14	12
Woods	6.0	7	65	29	42

SOURCE: Compiled from *Research Bulletin No. 17. State Test Results By Individual School for 1966, 1967, and 1968. A Technical Report of the Richmond Unified School District.* January 10, 1969.

Table A2. Relationship of School Site Size to
the Number of Pupils in Sample Schools in
the Suburbs, White Central City Neighborhoods, and the Black Ghetto in the RUSD

Schools	Acres	Students	Students per Acre
Suburban			
Kensington	20.3	594	
Mira Vista	17.2	834	
Valley View	14.0	281	
Ellerhorst	12.0	628	
TOTAL	63.5	2,337	36.8
White Central-city			
Dover	6.4	675	
Belding	4.7	689	
Broadway	4.0	445	
Ford	3.0	476	
TOTAL	18.1	2,285	125.1
Black			
Nystrom	6.9	695	
King	4.7	691	
Coronado	4.0	525	
Stege	3.9	482	
TOTAL	19.5	2,393	122.8

SOURCE: Compiled from data of the Richmond Unified School District, 1970.

Table A3. Annual Family Income, 1968.
San Pablo, Richmond, Contra Costa County

| | \multicolumn{5}{c}{Family Income} | | | | |
Area	Less than $3,000	$3,000–5,000	$5,000–8,000	$8,000–10,000	More than $10,000
San Pablo	16%	11%	27%	21%	26%
Richmond	17	10	22	19	32
Contra Costa County	14	8	20	19	39

SOURCE: San Pablo Planning Department, Survey of Buying Power, 1968.

NOTE: Examination of this table shows 48 percent of San Pablo's population in the $5,000–10,000 income bracket, compared to 41 percent in Richmond and 39 percent county-wide. Twenty-seven percent of San Pablo residents have incomes of less than $5,000, a figure exactly the same as Richmond's. But those figures must be understood in the context of the racial characteristics of the two cities. In 1960, when blacks accounted for 20 percent of Richmond's population, they were only 1 percent of San Pablo's. By 1966 Richmond's black population had increased to just under 30 percent of its total, and San Pablo's is estimated to have been no more than 2 percent. Thus, poverty in Richmond is dominantly black, whereas in San Pablo it is white.

Table A4. Racial Distribution of Pupils in
RUSD Elementary Schools, 1967–1970

School	Percentage of Black Pupils				Total Pupils
	Oct. 1967	Oct. 1968	Oct. 1969	Oct. 1970	Oct. 1970
Alvarado	13%	17%	22%	27%	438
Balboa	7	19	27	28	193
Bayview	18	19	21	24	720
Belding	4	5	13	16	689
Broadway	0	0	3	5	445
Cameron	10	19	17	23	60
Castro	2	2	7	10	505
Collins	0	0	3	3	553
Coronado	98	98	97	98	525
Cortez	74	85	89	93	398
Del Mar	8	7	11	20	376
Dover	3	2	10	11	675
Ellerhorst	0	0	0	2	628
El Monte	7	17	29	27	335
El Portal	6	7	10	12	488
El Sobrante	0	0	0	0	509
Fairmede	7	10	18	21	629
Fairmont	2	3	13	16	487
Ford	0	20	25	23	476
Grant	2	19	21	19	621
Harding	3	4	17	18	357
Hillview	2	1	4	4	248
Kensington	1	1	4	15	594
Kerry Hills	0	0	0	0	778
Lake	37	37	33	35	451
Lincoln	46	47	52	54	436
Madera	7	19	32	35	345
Mira Vista	5	8	14	20	834
Montalvin	0	0	1	2	665
Murphy	3	10	10	11	480
Nystrom	93	93	95	96	695
Olinda	0	0	0	6	233
Peres	93	91	92	93	746
King	93	94	95	94	691
Rancho	0	0	1	1	369
Riverside	6	8	12	14	491
Serra	3	3	7	13	265

Table A4. (continued) Racial Distribution
of Pupils in RUSD Elementary Schools,
1967–1970

School	Oct. 1967	Oct. 1968	Oct. 1969	Oct. 1970	Total Pupils Oct. 1970
	Percentage of Black Pupils				
Shannon	0	0	1	1	546
Sheldon	1	9	13	15	368
Stege	81	74	78	78	482
Stewart	0	0	2	1	555
Tara Hills	0	0	0	0	870
Valley View	0	0	2	3	281
Verde	98	97	98	99	332
Vista Hills	9	13	20	26	200
Washington	34	37	32	32	354
Wilson	2	9	10	13	503
Woods	6	7	13	18	390
All Elementary Schools	24.2	24.8	26.2	27.0	23,309

SOURCE: Richmond Unified School District

Table A5. Racial Distribution of Pupils in
RUSD Secondary Schools, 1967–1970

| School | Percentage of Black Pupils | | | | Total Pupils |
	Oct. 1967	Oct. 1968	Oct. 1969	Oct. 1970	Oct. 1970
Adams Jr. High	27%	29%	31%	35%	1,057
Crespi Jr. High	2	3	4	9	1,301
De Anza High	1	1	3	4	1,763
Downer Jr. High	25	28	33	42	923
El Cerrito High	11	13	20	24	1,650
Ells High	—	—	—	39	987
Helms Jr. High	26	27	30	38	1,143
Kennedy High	48	51	51	53	1,605
Pinole Jr. High	0	0	0	2	778
Pinole Valley High	7	6	4	4	1,874
Portola Jr. High	24	27	36	37	1,720
Richmond High	—	—	—	32	2,513
Richmond High (North)[a]	23	27	30	—	—
Richmond High (South)[a]	25	24	26	—	—
Roosevelt Jr. High[b]	70	75	78	—	—
All Secondary Schools	22.3	23.2	24.9	26.2	17,314

SOURCE: Richmond Unified School District.

[a] These two schools were consolidated into the new Richmond High in 1970.

[b] This School was closed in 1970.

Document 1. Occupational Rating Scale as used by the RUSD in 1968

Rating	Types of Occupation
1	Doctor, C.P.A., lawyer, engineer, architect, owner of a large business, marketing sales manager of a large business, airline pilot, high-ranking bureaucrat, corporate executive.
2	Teacher, journalist, registered nurse, accountant, owner of a medium size business, manager of a large store, investment broker, army colonel, auditor, real estate agent.
3	Draftsman, owner of a medium small business, medium small contractor, minor bureaucrat, secretary, bookkeeper, laboratory technician.
4	Owner of a small business, store clerk, stenographer, beautician, barber, army specialist, craftsman and any skilled worker (carpenter, mason, plumber, etc.), foreman, policeman.
5	Owner of a very small business, telephone worker, freight dispatcher.
6	Service station attendant, freight checker, truck driver, taxi driver, knitter, grinder, machine operator, semi-skilled operators, waitress, elevator operator, janitor.
7	Domestic worker, window washer, unskilled worker, laborer, factory production worker.
8	Welfare, unemployed.

SOURCE: A document of the Richmond Unified School District, 1968. This scale was designed by the research staff of the RUSD to classify data about the occupational level of students' families.

Document 2. Areas of Open Enrollment in the RUSD

Martin Luther King Elementary School
Mira Vista
Mira Vista Annex
Kensington
Riverside

Stege Elementary School
El Monte
Madera
Serra

Lincoln Elementary School
Grant
Wilson

Peres Elementary School
Ford
Murphy
Sheldon
Valley View
Hillview
Olinda

Cortez Elementary School
Castro
Del Mar

Coronado Elementary School
Fairmont
Harding

Nystrom Elementary School
Stewart
Collins

Verde Elementary School
El Portal
Fairmede
Vista Hills
Broadway
Rancho
Dover

Roosevelt Junior High School
Crespi
Downer
Helms
Portola

Kennedy Senior High School
De Anza
El Cerrito

SOURCE: A document of the Richmond Unified School District, July 1969.

Document 3. Suggested Rules and Regulations for
Open Enrollment in the RUSD

1. The registration period will be between August 4 and 15, 1969.
2. Parents will register their children at any junior high school in
    the district. The junior high schools will be open for that pur-
    pose from 9 A.M. to 8 P.M., with school district personnel present
    to register children.
3. Parents who select open enrollment will agree that their chil-
    dren will attend the receiving school for at least one full school
    year.
4. Any student who is involved in the open enrollment plan may
    return to his school of residence at the end of a school year, if
    his parents so desire.
5. No child may be returned to his area of residence school because
    of discipline problems.
6. Open enrollment must be used in a manner that is educationally
    sound. For example, no parent would be permitted to change a
    pupil's school each year.
7. ESEA and any other applicable Federal or state funds will fol-
    low the pupils to the schools they have selected, wherever such
    transfer of funds is permitted by law.

SOURCE: A document of the Richmond Unified School District,
July 1969.

NOTES

NOTES

CHAPTER 1

1. *Richmond Independent*, November 9, 1964.

CHAPTER 2

1. State of California Education Code, Section 17654, as amended by Stats. 1963, Ch. 2163 and Stats. 1963, Ch. 14.

2. Contra Costa County Committee on School District Organization, *Arguments For and Against Unification*.

3. Contra Costa County Committee on School District Organization, *Arguments*.

4. Pinole Chamber of Commerce and Pinole-Hercules school board president, as reported in the *Richmond Independent*, October 9, 1964, and October 12, 1964, respectively.

5. RUSD, *Minutes of the Meetings of the Board of Education*, August 17, 1966; September 15, 1967; June 5, 1968. The last date was before the June 30 fiscal deadline, but it was too late to call an election in time.

6. RUSD, *Minutes*, January 8, 1969; February 5, 1969; April 16, 1969.

7. RUSD, *Report of the Personnel Standards and Ethics Commission, California Association of School Administration, California School Boards Association, California Teachers Association*, November 1968; RUSD, Minutes, December 18, 1968.

8. RUSD, *Minutes*, April 3, 1967.

9. Kathleen Archibald, *Wartime Shipyard: A Study in Social Disunity*, p. 43.

10. Robert Wenkert, et al., *An Historical Digest of Negro-White Relations in Richmond, California*, p. 18.

11. Wenkert, *An Historical Digest*, p. 19.

12. Archibald, *Wartime Shipyard*, p. 62.

13. Archibald, *Wartime Shipyard*, pp. 48, 60–61, 80–84, 128–150.

14. Wenkert, *An Historical Digest*, p. 30.

15. Wenkert, *An Historical Digest*, p. 21.

16. Alan B. Wilson, *Western Contra Costa County Population, 1965: Demographic Characteristics*, p. 2.

CHAPTER 3

1. Daniel Bell, "Interpretation of American Politics" and "The Dispossessed"; Benjamin R. Epstein and Arnold Forster, *The Radical Right: Report on the John Birch Society and Its Allies*; Richard Hofstadter, *The Paranoid Style in American Politics*; Herbert H. Hyman, "England and America: Climates of Tolerance and Intolerance"; Robert E. Lane, *Political Ideology*; Seymour Martin Lipset, "The Sources of the 'Radical Right' " and "Three Decades of the Radical Right: Coughlinites, McCarthyites and Birchers"; Talcott Parsons, "Social Strains in America"; David Riesman and Nathan Glazer, "The Intellectuals and the Discontented Classes"; Edward A. Shils, "Authoritarianism: Right and Left"; Peter Viereck, "The Revolt Against the Elite" and "The Philosophical 'New Conservatism' "; Alan F. Westin, "The Birch Society."

2. Hofstadter, *The Paranoid Style*; Lipset, "The Sources" and "Three Decades." For a critical application of this concept, see Raymond E. Wolfinger, et al., "America's Radical Right: Politics and Ideology."

3. Edward C. Banfield and James Q. Wilson, *City Politics*; James Q. Wilson, "Planning and Politics: Citizen Participation in Urban Renewal."

4. Seymour Martin Lipset, *Political Man: The Social Bases of Politics*.

5. Hofstadter, *The Paranoid Style*, p. 82.

6. Bennett M. Berger, *Working-Class Suburb*, p. 23.

7. James S. Coleman, et al., *Equality of Educational Opportunity*.

8. Berger, *Working-Class*; Jessie Bernard, *Marriage and Family Among Negroes*; Peter Binzen, *Whitetown USA*; Imogene Cahill, "Child-Rearing Practices in Lower Socio-Economic Ethnic Groups"; Herbert J. Gans, *The Urban Villagers: Group and Class in the Life of Italian-Americans* and *The Levittowners*; Scott Greer, "Urbanization and Social Character: Notes on the American Citizen"; Alan L. Grey, ed., *Class and Personality in Society*; Gerald Handel and Lee Rainwater, "Persistence and Change in Working Class Life Style"; Mirra Komarovsky, *Blue Collar Marriage*; Lipset, *Political Man*; David Lockwood, "Sources of Variation in Working Class

Images of Society"; Leonard I. Pearlin and Melvin L. Kohn, "Social Class, Occupation, and Parental Values: A Cross-National Study"; Lee Rainwater, et al., *Workingman's Wife*; Lee Rainwater, "Work and Identity in the Lower Class"; Hyman Rodman, "The Lower-Class Value Stretch"; Arthur B. Shostak and William Gomberg, *Blue-Collar World: Studies of the American Worker*; Harold L. Wilensky, "Orderly Careers and Social Participation: The Impact of Work History on Social Integration of the Middle Mass," "Mass Society and Mass Culture: Interdependence or Independence," and "Class, Class Consciousness, and American Workers."

9. Louis Schneider and Sverre Lysgaard, "The Deferred Gratification Pattern: A Preliminary Study." For an excellent critique, see S. M. Miller, Frank Riessman, and Arthur A. Seagull, "Poverty and Self-Indulgence: A Critique of the Non-Deferred Gratification Pattern."

10. Allison Davis, "The Motivation of the Under-Privileged Worker"; Herbert Hyman, "The Value Systems of Different Classes: A Social Psychological Contribution to the Analysis of Stratification"; Genevieve Knupfer, "Portrait of the Underdog"; Oscar Lewis, *La Vida*; Elliot Liebow, *Tally's Corner*; Walter B. Miller, "Lower Class Culture as a Generating Milieu of Gang Delinquency"; Daniel P. Moynihan, *The Negro Family: The Case for National Action*. For critiques of this view, see: Laura Carper, "The Negro Family and the Moynihan Report"; Herbert J. Gans, "Culture and Class in the Study of Poverty: An Approach to Antipoverty Research," and "The Negro Family: Reflections on the Moynihan Report," in *People and Plans*; Thomas Gladwin, *Poverty USA*; Hylan Lewis, "Culture, Class and Family Life Among Low-Income Urban Negroes"; Bernard Mackler and Morsley G. Giddings, "Cultural Deprivation: A Study in Mythology"; S. M. Miller and Frank Riessman, "The Working-Class Subculture: A new View," and *Social Class and Social Policy*; Lee Rainwater, "Work and Identity" and "Crucible of Identity: The Negro Lower-Class Family"; Lee Rainwater and William L. Yancey, *The Moynihan Report and the Politics of Controversy*; Frank Riessman, "In Defense of the Negro Family"; Charles A. Valentine, *Culture and Poverty: Critique and Counter Proposals* and "Deficit, Difference and Bi-Cultural Models of Afro-American Behavior"; William L. Yancey, "The Culture of Poverty: Not So Much Parsimony."

11. Banfield and Wilson, *City*; Wilson, "Planning."

12. Wilson, "Planning," pp. 412–413.

13. Wilson, "Planning," pp. 413–414.

14. Wilson, "Planning," p. 414.

15. Melvin Tumin, "Captives, Consensus and Conflict: Implications for New Roles in Social Change."

16. Wilson, "Planning."

17. Lipset, *Political Man.*

18. For a perceptive analysis of class-related differences that fueled a school controversy in Levittown, see Gans, *The Levittowners.*

19. See Pearlin and Kohn, "Social Class," where they present some recent empirical evidence on this point. Also, for some discussions on work, alienation, and life style, see: Berger, *Working-Class*; Robert Blauner, *Alienation and Freedom: The Factory Worker and his Industry*; Eli Chinoy *Automobile Workers and The American Dream*; Robert Dubin, "Industrial Workers' World: A Study of the Central Life Interests of Industrial Workers"; John J. Goldthorpe, et al., *The Affluent Worker: Industrial Attitudes and Behavior*; Lewis Lipsitz, "Work Life and Political Attitudes: A Study of Manual Workers" and "On Political Belief: The Grievances of the Poor"; Lockwood, "Sources"; Charles R. Walker and Robert H. Guest, *The Man on the Assembly Line.*

20. Harold L. Wilensky, "The Moonlighter: A Product of Relative Deprivation."

21. Harvey Aronson, "Life with Cappelli on $101 a Week"; Pete Hamill, "The Revolt of the White Lower-Middle Class"; S. M. Miller, "Sharing the Burden of Change"; Brendon Sexton, "Workers and Liberals: Closing the Gap."

22. Cf. Gans, *The Urban Villagers.*

23. Robert A. Dentler and Constance Elkins, "Intergroup Attitudes, Academic Performance, and Racial Composition."

24. Michael P. Rogin, "Wallace and the Middle Class: The White Backlash in Wisconsin," and "Politics, Emotion, and the Wallace Vote."

25. Coleman et al., *Equality*; United States Commission on Civil Rights, *Racial Isolation in the Public Schools.*

26. RUSD, *Minutes of the Meetings of the Board of Education*, May 25, 1966, p. 180.

27. *Richmond Independent*, August 25, 1970.

28. Robin M. Williams, Jr., and Margaret W. Ryan, *Schools in Transition.*

29. Reginald G. Damerell, *Triumph in a White Suburb.*

CHAPTER 4

1. RUSD, *Memorandum*, August 23, 1967.

2. Cf. Annie Stein, "Strategies of Failure," where she argues that

institutional racism has consistently thwarted both desegregation and improvement in schooling in New York City.

3. Robert Wenkert, *An Historical Digest of Negro-White Relations in Richmond, California,* pp. 53–54.

4. RUSD, *Minutes of the Meetings of the Board of Education,* September 22, 1965, p. 43.

5. RUSD, *Minutes,* July 28, 1965, pp. 18–20.

6. Letter to the RUSD Board, November 18, 1965.

CHAPTER 5

1. Herbert J. Gans, *The Levittowners,* p. 309.

2. Citizen's Advisory Committee on DeFacto Segregation hearing, *Minutes,* January 27, 1967, p. 5.

3. Peter Bachrach, *The Theory of Democratic Elitism: A Critique,* p. 4.

4. Cf. Robert A. Dahl, *A Preface to Democratic Theory;* Andrew Hacker, ed., *The Federalist Papers.*

5. T. W. Adorno, et al., *The Authoritarian Personality;* Hannah Arendt, *The Origins of Totalitarianism;* Erich Fromm, *Escape from Freedom;* Emil Lederer, State of the Masses.

6. Adorno, et al., *The Authoritarian Personality.*

7. See John P. Kirscht and Ronald C. Dillehay, *Dimensions of Authoritarianism: A Review of Research and Theory.*

8. Robert A. Dahl, *Pluralist Democracy in the United States,* p. 261.

9. Bernard R. Berelson, et al., *Voting: A Study of Opinion Formation in a Presidential Campaign,* p. 313.

10. For one of the clearest and most concise statements of liberal pluralist elitism in the literature, see Edward A. Shils, *The Torment of Secrecy.* Also see Robert A. Dahl, *Who Governs?,* a study based on the pluralist model.

11. For typical statements, see William Kornhauser, *Politics of a Mass Society,* and David Truman, *Governmental Process.*

12. Kornhauser, *Politics;* Philip Selznick, *Leadership in Administration;* Truman, *Governmental.* For an excellent critique of this viewpoint, see Michael P. Rogin, *The Intellectuals and McCarthy: The Radical Specter.*

13. Edward C. Banfield and James Q. Wilson, *City Politics;* Berelson, et al., *Voting;* Kornhauser, *Politics;* Robert E. Lane, *Political Ideology;* Seymour Martin Lipset, *Political Man: the Social Bases of Politics;* Joseph A. Schumpeter, *Capitalism, Socialism and Democracy.*

14. See, for example, Berelson, et al., *Voting*; Dahl, *Who Governs?*; Truman, *Governmental*.

15. Berelson, et al., *Voting*, p. 312.

16. Banfield and Wilson, *City*; Berelson, et al., *Voting*; Lane, *Political Ideology*; Lipset, *Political Man*; Schumpeter, *Capitalism*; Shils, *The Torment*.

17. Melvin Tumin, "Captives Consensus and Conflict: Implications for New Roles in Social Change," p. 98.

18. Edmund Burke, *Reflections on the Revolution in France*; Thomas Hobbes, *Leviathan*; José Ortega y Gasset, *The Revolt of the Masses*.

19. For example: Arendt, *The Origins*; Emile Durkheim, *The Division of Labor in Society*; Kornhauser, *Politics*; Lederer, *State*; Shils, *The Torment*.

20. Daniel Bell, ed., *The Radical Right*; Philip E. Converse, "The Nature of Belief Systems in Mass Publics"; Richard Hofstadter, *The Age of Reform* and *The Paranoid Style in American Politics*; Lane, *Political Ideology*; Lipset, *Political Man*. For criticism of this approach see: William A. Gamson and James McEvoy, "Police Violence and Its Public Support"; Lewis Lipsitz, "Work Life and Political Attitudes: A Study of Manual Workers," and "On Political Belief"; Michael P. Rogin, *The Intellectuals and McCarthy: The Radical Specter*, "Politics and the Wallace Vote," and "Non-Partisanship and the Group Interest."

21. Raymond E. Callahan, *Education and the Cult of Efficiency*; Alan K. Campbell, "Who Governs the Schools?"; Michael Decker and Louis H. Masotti, "Determining the Quality of Education: A Political Process"; Jason Epstein, "The Politics of School Decentralization"; Mario Fantini, Marilyn Gittell, Richard Magat, *Community Control and the Urban School*; Marilyn Gittell and Alan G. Hevesi, *The Politics of Urban Education*; Michael B. Katz, *The Irony of Early School Reform: Educational Innovation in Mid-Nineteenth Century Massachusetts*; James D. Koerner, *Who Controls American Education?*; Robert H. Salisbury, "Autonomy vs. 'Political Control' of Schools."

22. RUSD, *Minutes of the Meetings of the Board of Education*, May 17, 1967, p. 218.

CHAPTER 6

1. RUSD, *The Report of the Citizens' Advisory Committee on DeFacto Segregation to the Board of Education*, p. 49.

CHAPTER 7

1. For an inside account, see Mark Peppard, "School Desegregation: A Case Study of Polarization Within a Community."
2. *La Tina Johnson, et al. vs. Richmond Unified School District, et al.*
3. RUSD, *Minutes of the Meetings of the Board of Education*, December 18, 1968, pp. 158–160.
4. RUSD, *Minutes*, February 7, 1968, pp. 180–181.
5. RUSD, *Minutes*, November 6, 1968, p. 122.
6. RUSD, *Minutes*, November 6, 1968, p. 122.

CHAPTER 8

1. Source: Contra Costa County Superintendent of Schools.
2. *Richmond Independent*, February 13 and April 4, 1969.
3. *Richmond Independent*, March 29 and April 11, 1969.
4. *Richmond Independent*, April 6, 1969.
5. Alan B. Wilson, *Western Contra Costa County Population, 1965. Demographic Characteristics.*

CHAPTER 9

1. CEE Policy Statement, *Richmond Independent*, June 28, 1969.
2. RUSD, *Minutes of the Meetings of the Board of Education*, June 4, 1969.

CHAPTER 10

1. RUSD, *Minutes of the Meetings of the Board of Education*, July 1, 1969, p. 3.
2. RUSD, *Minutes*, August 20, 1969.
3. RUSD, board meeting August 20, 1969.
4. RUSD, *Minutes*, October 1, 1969.
5. Willmoore Kendall, *The Conservative Affirmation*, p. 55.

CHAPTER 11

1. For a recent analysis of a national sample and a review of the literature, see Gertrude J. Selznick and Stephen Steinberg, *The Tenacity of Prejudice*.
2. Martin Meyerson and Edward C. Banfield, *Politics, Planning, and the Public Interest*, p. 253.

3. Gordon W. Allport, *The Nature of Prejudice*, p. v.

4. Reginald G. Damerell, *Triumph in a White Suburb*, p. 336.

5. *Seattle Post-Intelligencer*, October 2, 1971.

6. Michael P. Rogin, *The Intellectuals and McCarthy: The Radical Specter*, p. 268.

7. Melvin Tumin, "Captives, Consensus and Conflict," p. 111.

8. Aaron V. Cicourel and John I. Kitsuse, *The Educational Decision-Makers*; Kenneth B. Clark, *Dark Ghetto*; James S. Coleman, et al., *Equality of Educational Opportunity*; George Dennison, *The Lives of Children*; Robert A. Dentler, et al., eds., *The Urban R's*; Harvard Education Review, eds., *Equal Educational Opportunity*; Nat Hentoff, *Our Children Are Dying*; James Herndon, *The Way It Spozed to Be*; August B. Hollingshead, *Elmtown's Youth*; John Holt, *How Children Fail* and *How Children Learn*; Herbert Kohl, *Teaching the "Unteachable"* and *Thirty-six Children*; Jonathan Kozol, *Death at an Early Age*; Eleanor Burke Leacock, *Teaching and Learning in City Schools*; S. M. Miller and Frank Riessman, *Social Class and Social Policy*; A Harvey Passow, eds., *Education in Depressed Areas*; Robert Rosenthal and Lenore Jacobson, *Pygmalion in the Classroom*; Walter E. Schafer, et al., "Programmed for Social Class: Tracking in High School"; Peter Schrag, *Village School Downtown*; Patricia Cayo Sexton, *Education and Income* and *The American School*; David Street, ed., *Innovation in Mass Education*; United States Commission on Civil Rights, *Racial Isolation in the Public Schools*; Alan B. Wilson, "Residential Segregation of Social Classes and Aspirations of High School Boys," *Educational Consequences of Segregation in a California Community*, and "Social Class and Equal Educational Opportunity.

9. John Sharnik, "When Things Go Wrong All Blacks Are Black and All Whites Are Whitey."

10. For an excellent and lucid discussion, see Philip Green, "Decentralization, Community Control, and Revolution: Reflections on Ocean Hill-Brownsville."

BIBLIOGRAPHY

Adorno, T. W., et al., 1950. *The Authoritarian Personality.* New York: Harper & Brothers.

Allport, Gordon W. 1958. *The Nature of Prejudice.* New York: Doubleday, Anchor.

Archibald, Kathleen. 1947. *Wartime Shipyard: A Study in Social Disunity.* Berkeley and Los Angeles: University of California Press.

Arendt, Hannah. 1958. *The Origins of Totalitarianism.* New York: World, Meridian.

Aronson, Harvey. 1970. "Life with Cappelli on $101 a Week." In *The White Majority*, ed. Louise Kapp Howe, pp. 25–34. New York: Random House, Vintage.

Bachrach, Peter. 1967. *The Theory of Democratic Elitism: A Critique.* Boston: Little, Brown.

Banfield, Edward C., and Wilson, James Q. 1963. *City Politics.* Cambridge: Harvard University Press.

Bell, Daniel, ed. 1964. *The Radical Right.* New York: Doubleday, Anchor.

————. 1964. "The Dispossessed" (1962). In *The Radical Right*, ed. Daniel Bell, pp. 1–45. New York: Doubleday, Anchor.

————. 1964. "Interpretation of American Politics" (1955). In *The Radical Right*, ed. Daniel Bell, pp. 47–73. New York: Doubleday, Anchor.

Bennett, Jr., Lerone. 1966. "The White Problem in America." In *The White Problem in America*, ed. Ebony, pp. 13–22. New York: Lancer.

Berelson, Bernard R., et al. 1954. *Voting: A Study of Opinion Formation in a Presidential Campaign.* Chicago: University of Chicago Press.

Berger, Bennett M. 1960. *Working-Class Suburb.* Berkeley and Los Angeles: University of California Press.

Bernard, Jessie. 1966. *Marriage and Family Among Negroes.* Englewood Cliffs, N.J. Prentice-Hall.

Binzen, Peter. 1970. *Whitetown USA.* New York: Random House.

Blauner, Robert. 1964. *Alienation and Freedom: The Factory Worker and His Industry.* Chicago: University of Chicago Press.

———. 1966. "Work Satisfaction and Industrial Trends in Modern Society." in *Class, Status, and Power,* eds. Reinhard Bendix and Seymour Martin Lipset, pp. 473–481. Second edition. New York: Free Press.

Boggs, James. 1970. "A Black View of the White Worker." In *The White Majority,* ed. Louise Kapp Howe, pp. 103–110. New York: Random House, Vintage.

Bottomore, Tom. 1970. "Conservative Man." *The New York Review of Books* 15 (October 8):21ff.

Bowles, Samuel. 1969. "Toward Equality of Educational Opportunity." In *Equal Educational Opportunity,* pp. 115–125. Cambridge: Harvard University Press.

Burke, Edmund. 1961. *Reflections on the Revolution in France.* New York: Doubleday, Dolphin.

Cahill, Imogene. 1967. "Child-Rearing Practices in Lower Socio-Economic Ethnic Groups." In *The Urban R's,* ed. Robert A. Dentler, et al, pp. 268–287. New York: Frederick A. Praeger.

Callahan, Raymond E. 1962. *Education and the Cult of Efficiency.* Chicago: University of Chicago Press.

Campbell, Alan K. 1968. "Who Governs the Schools?" *Saturday Review* 51 (December 21):50ff.

Carper, Laura. 1968. "The Negro Family and the Moynihan Report." In *Poverty Views from the Left,* eds. Jeremy Larner and Irving Howe, pp. 196–205. New York: William Morrow.

Chinoy, Eli. 1965. *Automobile Workers and the American Dream.* Boston: Beacon Press.

Cicourel, Aaron V., and Kitsuse, John I. 1963. *The Educational Decision-Makers.* Indianapolis: Bobbs-Merrill.

Clark, Kenneth B. 1963. "Educational Stimulation of Racially Disadvantaged Children." In *Education in Depressed Areas,* ed. A. Harvey Passow, pp. 142–162. New York: Teachers College Press.

———. 1965. *Dark Ghetto.* New York: Harper & Row.

Cohen, David K. 1969. "Policy for the Public Schools: Compensation and Integration." In *Equal Educational Opportunity,* pp. 91–114. Cambridge, Harvard University Press.

Coleman, James S., et al. 1966. *Equality of Educational Opportunity.* Washington, D.C.: U.S. Government Printing Office.

Contra Costa County Committee on School District Organization. 1964. *Arguments For and Against Unification.*

Converse, Philip E. 1964. "The Nature of Belief Systems in Mass Publics." In *Ideology and Discontent,* ed. David Apter, pp. 206–261. New York: Free Press.

Crain, Robert L., et al. 1969. *The Politics of School Desegregation.* New York: Doubleday, Anchor.

Dahl, Robert A. 1956. *A Preface to Democratic Theory.* Chicago: University of Chicago Press.

————. 1961. *Who Governs?* New Haven: Yale University Press.

————. 1967. *Pluralist Democracy in the United States.* Chicago: Rand McNally.

Damerell, Reginald G. 1968. *Triumph in a White Suburb.* New York: William Morrow.

Davis, Allison. 1946. "The Motivation of the Under-Privileged Worker." In *Industry and Society*, ed. William Foote Whyte, pp. 84–106. New York: McGraw-Hill.

Decker, Michael, and Masotti, Louis H. 1969. "Determining the Quality of Education: A Political Process." In *The Quality of Urban Life*, eds. Henry J. Schmandt and Warner Bloomberg, Jr., pp. 355–373. Beverly Hills: Sage Publications.

Dennison, George. 1969. *The Lives of Children.* New York: Random House, Vintage.

Dentler, Robert A., et al, eds. 1967. *The Urban R's.* New York: Frederick A. Praeger.

———— and Elkins, Constance. 1967. "Intergroup Attitudes, Academic Performance, and Racial Composition." In *The Urban R's*, ed. Robert A. Dentler, et al., pp. 61–77. New York: Frederick A. Praeger.

Dubin, Robert. 1956. "Industrial Workers' World: A Study of the Central Life Interests of Industrial Workers." *Social Problems* 3 (January):131–141.

Durkheim, Emile. 1964. *The Division of Labor in Society.* New York: Free Press.

Duster, Troy. 1968. "Violence and Civic Responsibility: Combinations of 'Fear' and 'Right.' " In *Our Children's Burden*, ed. Raymond W. Mack, pp. 1–39. New York: Random House, Vintage.

Dwyer, Henry S. 1969. "School Factors and Equal Educational Opportunity." In *Equal Educational Opportunity*, ed. Harvard Educational Review, pp. 41–59. Cambridge: Harvard University Press.

Epstein, Benjamin R., and Forster, Arnold. 1967. *The Radical Right: Report on the John Birch Society and Its Allies.* New York: Random House, Vintage.

Epstein, Jason. 1968. "The Politics of School Decentralization." *New York Review of Books* 10 (June 6):26–32.

————. 1968. "The Brooklyn Dodgers." *New York Review of Books* 11 (October 10):37–41.

————. 1968. "The Issue at Ocean Hill." *New York Review of Books* 11 (November 21):3ff.

Fantini, Mario; Gittell, Marilyn; Magat, Richard. 1970. *Community Control and the Urban School.* New York: Frederick A. Praeger.

Fein, Leonard J. 1970. "The Limits of Liberalism." *Saturday Review* 53 (June 20):83ff.

Fromm, Erich. 1941. *Escape from Freedom.* New York: Avon.

Gamson, William A., and McEvoy, James. 1970. "Police Violence and Its Public Support." *Annals of the American Academy of Political and Social Science* 391 (September):97–110.

Gans, Herbert J. 1962. *The Urban Villagers: Group and Class in the Life of Italian-Americans.* New York: Free Press.

———. 1967. *The Levittowners.* New York: Pantheon.

———. 1968. *People and Plans.* New York: Basic Books.

Gittell, Marilyn. 1969. "Professionalism and Public Participation in Educational Policy Making: New York City, a Case Study." In *The Politics of Urban Education*, eds. Marilyn Gittell and Alan G. Hevesi, pp. 155–177. New York: Frederick A. Praeger.

——— and Hevesi, Alan G., eds. 1969. *The Politics of Urban Education.* New York: Frederick A. Praeger.

Gladwin, Thomas. 1967. *Poverty, USA.* Boston: Little, Brown.

Goldthorpe, John H., et al. 1968. *The Affluent Worker: Industrial Attitudes and Behavior.* Cambridge: Cambridge University Press.

Gordon, Sol. 1967. "Primary Education in Urban Slums: A Mental Health Orientation." In *The Urban R's*, eds. Robert A. Dentler, et al., pp. 189–204. New York: Frederick A. Praeger.

Gouldner, Alvin W. 1957. "Cosmopolitans and Locals: Toward an Analysis of Latent Social Roles (pt. 1). *Administrative Science Quarterly* 2 (December):281–306.

———. 1958. "Cosmopolitans and Locals: Toward an Analysis of Latent Social Roles (pt. 2). *Administrative Science Quarterly* 2 (March): 444–480.

Greeley, Andrew M. 1970. "White Against White: The Enduring Ethnic Conflict." In *The White Majority*, ed. Louise Kapp Howe, pp. 111–118. New York: Random House, Vintage.

Green, Philip. 1970. "Decentralization, Community Control, and Revolution: Reflections on Ocean Hill-Brownsville." In *Power and Community*, eds. Philip Green and Sanford Levinson, pp. 247–275. New York: Random House, Vintage.

——— and Levinson, Sanford, eds. 1970. *Power and Community: Dissenting Essays in Political Science.* New York: Random House, Vintage.

Greer, Scott. 1969. "Urbanization and Social Character: Notes on the American Citizen." In *The Quality of Urban Life*, ed. Henry J. Schmandt and Warner Bloomberg, Jr., pp. 95–127. Beverly Hills: Sage Publications.

Grey, Alan L., ed. 1969. *Class and Personality in Society*. New York: Atherton Press.

Hacker, Andrew, ed. 1964. *The Federalist Papers*. New York: Washington Square Press.

———. 1970. "Is There a New Republican Majority?" In *The White Majority*, ed. Louise Kapp Howe, pp. 263–278. New York: Random House, Vintage.

Hamill, Pete. 1970. "The Revolt of the White Lower-Middle Class." In *The White Majority*, ed. Louise Kapp Howe, pp. 10–24. New York: Random House, Vintage.

Handel, Gerald, and Rainwater, Lee. 1964. "Persistence and Change in Working Class Life Style." In *Blue-Collar World*, eds. Arthur B. Shostak and William Gomberg, pp. 36–41. Englewood Cliffs, N.J.: Prentice-Hall.

Harvard Education Review, eds. 1969. *Equal Educational Opportunity*. Cambridge: Harvard University Press.

Havighurst, Robert J., and Levine, Daniel U. 1969. "The Quality of Urban Education." In *The Quality of Urban Life*, ed. Henry J. Schmandt and Warner Bloomberg, Jr., pp. 323–354. Beverly Hills: Sage Publications.

Hentoff, Nat. 1966. *Our Children Are Dying*. New York: Viking Press.

Herndon, James. 1965. *The Way It Spozed to Be*. New York: Simon & Schuster.

Hobbes, Thomas. 1964. *Leviathan*. New York: Washington Square Press.

Hofstadter, Richard. 1955. *The Age of Reform*. New York: Random House, Vintage.

———. 1965. *The Paranoid Style in American Politics*. New York: Alfred A. Knopf.

Hollingshead, August B. 1949. *Elmtown's Youth*. New York: John Wiley.

Holt, John. 1970. *How Children Fail*. New York: Dell, Delta.

———. 1967. *How Children Learn*. New York: Pitman.

Howe, Louise Kapp, ed. 1970. *The White Majority: Between Poverty and Affluence*. New York: Random House, Vintage.

Hunt, J. McV. 1969. "Has Compensatory Education Failed? Has It Been Attempted?" *Harvard Educational Review* 39 (Spring): 130–151.

Hyman, Herbert H. 1953. "The Value Systems of Different Classes: A Social Psychological Contribution to the Analysis of Stratification." In *Class, Status, and Power*, eds. Reinhard Bendix and Seymour Martin Lipset, pp. 426–442. New York: Free Press.

———. 1964. "England and America: Climates of Tolerance and

Intolerance" (1962). In *The Radical Right*, ed. Daniel Bell. New York: Doubleday, Anchor.

Katz, Michael B. 1968. *The Irony of Early School Reform: Educational Innovation in Mid-Nineteenth Century Massachusetts.* Cambridge: Harvard University Press.

————. 1971. "The Present Movement in Educational Reform," *Harvard Educational Review* 41 (August): 342–359.

Kendall, Willmoore. 1963. *The Conservative Affirmation.* Chicago: Henry Regnery.

Kirscht, John P., and Dillehay, Ronald C. 1967. *Dimensions of Authoritarianism: A Review of Research and Theory.* Lexington: University of Kentucky Press.

Knupfer, Genevieve. 1947. "Portrait of the Underdog," *Public Opinion Quarterly* 11 (Spring): 103–114.

Koerner, James D. 1968. *Who Controls American Education?* Boston: Beacon Press.

Kohl, Herbert R. 1967. *Teaching the "Unteachable."* New York: New York Review.

————. 1968. *Thirty-six Children.* New York: New American Library, Signet.

Komarovsky, Mirra. 1962. *Blue Collar Marriage.* New York: Random House, Vintage.

Kornhauser, William. 1959. *Politics of a Mass Society.* New York: Free Press.

Kozol, Jonathan. 1967. *Death at an Early Age.* Boston: Houghton Mifflin.

Lane, Robert E. 1962. *Political Ideology.* New York: Free Press.

————. 1970. "The Fear of Equality." In *The White Majority*, ed Louise Kapp Howe, pp. 119–147. New York: Random House, Vintage.

La Tina Johnson, et al. vs. Richmond Unified School District, et al. 1969. Reporter's transcript of proceedings from the Superior Court of Contra Costa County, State of California. Honorable Robert J. Cooney, Judge.

Law and Society Association. 1967. *Affirmative Integration: Studies of Efforts to Overcome De Facto Segregation in the Public Schools. Law and Society Review* 2 (November).

Leacock, Eleanor Burke. 1969. *Teaching and Learning in City Schools.* New York: Basic Books.

Lederer, Emil. 1940. *State of the Masses.* New York: W. W. Morton.

Lerner, Michael. 1970. "Respectable Bigotry." In *The White Majority: Between Poverty and Affluence*, ed. Louise Kapp Howe, pp. 193–208. New York: Random House, Vintage.

Lewis, Hylan. 1967. "Culture, Class and Family Life Among Low-

Income Urban Negroes." In *Employment, Race, and Poverty,* eds. Arthur N. Ross and Herbert Hill, pp. 149–172. New York: Harcourt Brace & World.

Lewis, Oscar. 1968. *La Vida.* New York: Random House, Vintage.

Liebow, Elliot. 1966. *Tally's Corner.* Boston: Little, Brown.

Lipset, Seymour Martin. 1963. *Political Man: The Social Bases of Politics.* New York: Doubleday, Anchor.

——. 1964. "The Sources of the 'Radical Right' " (1955). In *The Radical Right,* ed. Daniel Bell, pp. 307–372. New York: Doubleday, Anchor.

——. 1964. "Three Decades of the Radical Right: Coughlinites, McCarthyites and Birchers" (1962). In *The Radical Right,* ed. Daniel Bell, pp. 373–446. New York: Doubleday, Anchor.

—— and Raab, Earl. 1970. "The Wallace Whitelash." In *The White Majority,* ed. Louise Kapp Howe, pp. 209–229. New York: Random House, Vintage.

Lipsitz, Lewis. 1970. "Work Life and Political Attitudes: A Study of Manual Workers." In *The White Majority,* ed. Louise Kapp Howe, pp. 148–170. New York: Random House, Vintage.

——. 1970. "On Political Belief: The Grievances of the Poor." In *Power and Community,* eds. Philip Green and Sanford Levinson, pp. 142–172. New York: Random House, Vintage.

Lockwood, David. 1966. "Sources of Variation in Working Class Images of Society." *Sociological Review* (November): 249–267.

Mack, Raymond W., ed. 1968. *Our Children's Burden.* New York: Random House, Vintage.

Mackler, Bernard, and Giddings, Morsley G. 1967. "Cultural Deprivation: A Study in Mythology." In *The Urban R's,* ed. Robert A. Dentler, pp. 208–214. New York: Frederick A. Praeger.

Mankoff, Milton. 1970. "Power in Advanced Capitalist Society: A Review Essay on Recent Elitist and Marxist Criticism of Pluralist Theory." *Social Problems* 17 (Winter):418–430.

Merton, Robert K. 1959. Patterns of Influence: Local and Cosmopolitan Influentials." In *Social Theory and Social Structure.* Revised and enlarged edition, pp. 387–420. New York: Free Press.

Meyerson, Martin, and Banfield, Edward C. 1955. *Politics, Planning, and the Public Interest.* New York: Free Press.

Miller, S. M. 1970. "Sharing the Burden of Change." In *The White Majority,* ed. Louise Kapp Howe, pp. 279–294. New York: Random House, Vintage.

Miller, S. M., and Riessman, Frank. 1961. "Working Class Authoritarianism: A Critique of Lipset." *British Journal of Sociology* (September): 263–276.

——. 1964. "The Working Class Subculture: A New View." In

Blue-Collar World, ed. Arthur B. Shostak and William Gomberg, pp. 24–35. Englewood Cliffs, N.J., Prentice-Hall, Inc.

—————. 1968. *Social Class and Social Policy*. New York: Basic Books.

————— and Seagull, Arthur A. 1965. "Poverty and Self-Indulgence: A Critique of the Non-Deferred Gratification Pattern." In *Poverty in America*, eds. Louis A. Ferman, et al., pp. 285–302. Ann Arbor: University of Michigan Press.

Miller, Walter B. 1958. "Lower Class Culture as a Generating Milieu of Gang Delinquency." *Journal of Social Issues* 14:5–19.

Moody, Kim. 1970. "Can the American Worker Be Radicalized?" In *The White Majority*, ed. Louise Kapp Howe, pp. 246–262. New York: Random House, Vintage.

Moynihan, Daniel P. 1965. *The Negro Family: The Case for National Action*. Washington, D.C.: U.S. Department of Labor.

Ortega y Gasset, José. 1957. *The Revolt of the Masses*. New York: W. W. Norton.

Parker, Richard. 1970. "The Myth of Middle America." *Center* 3 (March): 61–70.

Parsons, Talcott. 1964. "Social Strains in America (1955)," In *The Radical Right*, ed. Daniel Bell, pp. 209–230. New York: Doubleday, Anchor.

Passow, A. Harvey, ed. 1963. *Education in Depressed Areas*. New York: Teachers College Press.

Pearlin, Leonard I., and Kohn, Melvin L. 1969. "Social Class, Occupation, and Parental Values: A Cross-National Study." In *Class and Personality in Society*, ed. Alan L. Grey, pp. 161–183. New York: Atherton Press.

Pease, John; Form, William H.; and Rytina, Joan Huber, 1970. "Ideological Currents in American Stratification Literature." *American Sociologist* (May):127–137.

Peppard, Mark. 1969. "School Desegregation: A Case Study of Polarization Within a Community." Unpublished paper prepared at Boalt Hall School of Law, University of California, Berkeley.

Perrucci, Robert, and Pilisuk, Mark. 1969. "Leaders and Ruling Elites: The Interorganizational Basis of Community Power." Paper presented to the 64th Annual Meeting of the American Sociological Association, San Francisco.

Rainwater, Lee. 1964. "Work and Identity in the Lower Class." Mimeographed.

—————. 1966. "Crucible of Identity: The Negro Lower-Class Family." *Daedalus* 95 (Winter):172–216.

————— et al. 1962. *Workingman's Wife*. New York: Macfadden.

————— and Yancey, William L. 1967. *The Moynihan Report and the Politics of Controversy.* Cambridge: M.I.T. Press.

Richmond Unified School District 1965–1971. *Minutes of the Meetings of the Board of Education.*

—————. 1967. *The Report of the Citizens' Advisory Committee on De Facto Segregation to the Board of Education of the Richmond Unified School District.*

—————. 1968. *Report of the Personnel Standards and Ethics Commission, California Association of School Administration, California School Boards Association, California Teachers Association.*

—————. 1969. *Research Bulletin No. 17, State Test Results By Individual School for 1966, 1967 and 1968. A Technical Report.*

Riesman, David. 1964. "The Intellectuals and the Discontented Classes" (1962). In *The Radical Right,* ed. Daniel Bell, pp. 137–160. New York: Doubleday, Anchor.

————— and Glazer, Nathan. 1964. "The Intellectuals and the Discontented Classes" (1955). In *The Radical Right,* ed. Daniel Bell, pp. 137–160. New York: Doubleday, Anchor.

Riessman, Frank. 1962. *The Culturally Deprived Child.* New York: Harper & Brothers.

—————. 1966. "In Defense of the Negro Family." *Dissent* (March–April).

Roberts, Wallace. 1968. "The Battle for Urban Schools." *Saturday Review* 51 (November 16):97ff.

Rodman, Hyman. 1965. "The Lower-Class Value Stretch." In *Poverty in America,* eds. Louis A. Ferman, et al., pp. 270–285. Ann Arbor: University of Michigan Press.

Rogers, David. 1968. *110 Livingston Street.* New York: Random House.

Rogin, Michael P. 1966. "Wallace and the Middle Class: The White Backlash in Wisconsin." *Public Opinion Quarterly* 30 (Spring): 98–108.

—————. 1967. *The Intellectuals and McCarthy: The Radical Specter.* Cambridge: M.I.T. Press.

—————. 1969. "Politics, Emotion, and the Wallace Vote." *British Journal of Sociology* 20 (March):27–49.

—————. 1970. "Non-Partisanship and the Group Interest." In *Power and Community,* eds. Philip Green and Sanford Levinson, pp. 112–141. New York: Random House, Vintage.

————— and Shover, John L. 1969. *Political Change in California: Critical Elections and Social Movements, 1890–1966,* pp. 153–212. Westport, Conn. Greenwood Publishing Co.

Rose, Arnold. 1967. "School Desegregation: A Sociologist's View." *Law and Society Review* 2 (November):125–140.

Rosenthal, Robert, and Jacobson, Lenore. 1968. *Pygmalion in the Classroom.* New York: Holt, Rinehart & Winston.

Salisbury, Robert H. 1969. "Autonomy vs. 'Political Control' of Schools." In *Urban Government: A Reader in Administration and Politics,* ed. Edward C. Banfield, pp. 628–644. New York: Free Press.

Schafer, Walter E., et al. 1970. "Programmed for Social Class: Tracking in High School." *Trans-Action* 7 (October):39–46.

Schneider, Louis, and Lysgaard, Sverre. 1953. "The Deferred Gratification Pattern: A Preliminary Study." *American Sociological Review* 18 (April):142–149.

Schrag, Peter. 1968. *Village School Downtown.* Boston: Beacon Press.

Schumpter, Joseph A. 1962. *Capitalism, Socialism, and Democracy.* New York: Harper & Row, Torchbooks.

Scott, John Finley, and Scott, Lois Heyman. 1968. "They Are Not So Much Anti-Negro as Pro-Middle Class," *New York Times Magazine* (March 25): 46ff.

Selznick, Gertrude J., and Steinberg, Stephen. 1969. *The Tenacity of Prejudice.* New York: Harper & Row.

Selznick, Philip. 1957. *Leadership in Administration.* New York: Harper & Row.

Sennett, Richard. 1970. "The Brutality of Modern Families." *Trans-Action* 7 (September):29–37.

―――. 1970. *Families Against the City: Middle Class Homes of Industrial Chicago 1872–1890.* Cambridge: Harvard University Press.

Sexton, Brendon. 1970. "Workers and Liberals: Closing the Gap." In *The White Majority,* ed. Louise Kapp Howe, pp. 230–245. New York: Random House, Vintage.

Sexton, Patricia Cayo. 1964. *Education and Income.* New York: Viking.

―――. 1967. *The American School.* Englewood Cliffs, N.J.: Prentice-Hall.

Shanker, Albert. 1969. "What's Wrong with Compensatory Education?" *Saturday Review* January 11.

Sharnik, John. 1969. "When Things Go Wrong All Blacks Are Black and All Whites Are Whitey." *New York Times Magazine* (May 25).

Sherwin, Mark. 1963. *The Extremists.* New York: St. Martin's Press.

Shils, Edward A. 1954. "Authoritarianism: Right and Left." In *Studies in the Scope and Method of Authoritarian Personality,* eds.

Richard Christie and Marie Jahoda, pp. 24–49. New York: Free Press.

⸻. 1956. *The Torment of Secrecy.* New York: Free Press.

Shostak, Arthur B., and Gomberg, William. 1964. *Blue-Collar World: Studies of the American Worker.* Englewood Cliffs, N.J.: Prentice-Hall.

Silberman, Charles E. 1970. *Crisis in the Classroom.* New York: Random House.

Stein, Annie. 1971. "Strategies of Failure." *Harvard Educational Review* 41 (May):158–204.

Street, David, ed. 1969. *Innovation in Mass Education.* New York: John Wiley.

Truman, David. 1951. *Governmental Press.* New York: Alfred A. Knopf.

⸻. 1959. "The American System in Crisis." *Political Science Quarterly* December: 481–497.

Tumin, Melvin. 1968. "Captives, Consensus and Conflict: Implications for New Roles in Social Change." In *Social Theory and Social Invention,* ed. Herman D. Stein, pp. 93–113. Cleveland: The Press of Case Western Reserve University.

United States Commission on Civil Rights. 1967. *Racial Isolation in the Public Schools.* Washington, D.C.: U.S. Government Printing Office.

Valentine, Charles A. 1968. *Culture and Poverty: Critique and Counter Proposals.* Chicago: University of Chicago Press.

⸻. 1971. "Deficit, Difference, and Bicultural Models of Afro-American Behavior." *Harvard Educational Review* 41 (May): 137–157.

Vidich, Arthur J. and Bensman, Joseph. 1958. *Small Town in Mass Society.* New York: Doubleday, Anchor.

Viereck, Peter. 1964. "The Revolt Against the Elite" (1955). In *The Radical Right,* ed. Daniel Bell, pp. 161–184. New York: Doubleday, Anchor.

⸻. 1964. "The Philosophical 'New Conservatism'" (1962). In *The Radical Right,* ed. Daniel Bell, pp. 185–208. New York: Doubleday, Anchor.

Walker, Charles R., and Guest, Robert H. 1952. *The Man on the Assembly Line.* Cambridge: Harvard University Press.

Walker, Jack L. 1969. "A Critique of the Elitist Theory of Democracy." In *The Politics of Urban Education,* eds. Marilyn Gittell and Alan G. Hevesi, pp. 63–80. New York: Frederick A. Praeger.

Wenkert, Robert, et al. 1967. *An Historical Digest of Negro-White Relations in Richmond, California.* Berkeley: Survey Research Center, University of California.

————. 1967. *Two Weeks of Racial Crisis in Richmond, California*. Berkeley: Survey Research Center, University of California.

Werthman, Carl, et al. 1965. *Planning and the Purchase Decision: Why People Buy in Planned Communities*. Berkeley: Institute of Urban and Regional Planning, University of California.

Westin, Alan F. 1964. "The Birch Society" (1962). In *The Radical Right*, ed. Daniel Bell, pp. 239–268. New York: Doubleday, Anchor.

Wilensky, Harold L. 1961. "Orderly Careers and Social Participation: The Impact of Work History on Social Integration in the Middle Mass." *American Sociological Review* 26 (August):521–539.

————. 1963. "The Moonlighter: A Product of Relative Deprivation." *Industrial Relations* 3 (October):105–124.

————. 1964. "Mass Society and Mass Culture: Interdependence or Independence." *Amercan Sociological Review* 29 (April):173–197.

————. 1966. "Class, Class Consciousness, and American Workers." In *Labor in a Changing America*, ed. William Haber, pp. 12–44. New York: Basic Books.

Williams, Robin M., Jr., and Ryan, Margaret W. 1954. *Schools in Transition*. Chapel Hill: University of North Carolina Press.

Wilson, Alan B. 1959. "Residential Segregation of Social Classes and Aspirations of High School Boys." *American Sociological Review* 24 (December):836–845.

————. 1964. "A Social Area Analysis of Western Contra Costa County." Unpublished manuscript.

————. 1966. *Western Contra Costa County Population, 1965. Demographic Characteristics*. Berkeley: Survey Research Center, University of California.

————. 1967. *Educational Consequences of Segregation in a California Community*. Berkeley: Survey Research Center, University of California.

——————. 1969. "Social Class and Equal Educational Opportunity." In *Equal Educational Opportunity*, ed. *Harvard Educational Review*, pp. 80–87. Cambridge: Harvard University Press.

Wilson, James Q. 1966. "Planning and Politics: Citizen Participation in Urban Renewal." In *Urban Renewal: The Record and the Controversy*, ed. James Q. Wilson, pp. 407–421. Cambridge: M.I.T. Press.

———— and Banfield, Edward C. 1964. "Public-Regardingness as a Value Premise in Voting Behavior." *American Political Science Review* 58 (December):876–888.

Wolfinger, Raymond E., et al. 1964. "America's Radical Right: Politics and Ideology." In *Ideology and Discontent*, ed. David Apter, pp. 262–293. New York: Free Press.

Yancey, William L. n.d. "The Culture of Poverty: Not So Much Parsimony." Mimeographed.

Young, Michael, and Willmott, Peter. 1962. *Family and Kinship in East London*. Harmondsworth, England: Penguin Books.

INDEX

Allport, Gordon, 200

Anti-busing amendments, U.S. Congress, 5; Representative John Conyer, 6; Representative Edith Green, 6; Representative Shirley Chisolm, 6

Archibald, Kathleen, 35

Association of Richmond Educators (ARE), 140n, 141, 158, 158n

Authoritarian personality, 101, 103

Banfield, Edward, 46

Bartels, Don, 145

Barusch, Maurice, 126, 132

Belding School, optional attendance area, 79

Berelson, Bernard, 102, 103, 104

Berger, Bennett, 41

Berkeley, attitude toward, 7, 71, 92, 97, 115, 183

Berry, Margaret, 94, 132

Birch Society, John, 108–109, 134, 177

Black Caucus, 144

Black Crescent, 36, 82, 149

Broadway School, 128, 130, 132

Brown *vs.* Board of Education, 200

B-V-D plan, 130, 146

Cairo, Illinois, 72

Campaign finances (1969), 145–146

Candidate selection: 1967, 109; 1969, 143–144, 145

Censorship, 178, 180–181

Chicago, Hyde Park-Kenwood district, 48–49

Citizens Advisory Committee on De Facto Segregation (CACDFS): appointment of, 86–88, 199; hearings, 90–93, 128; structure of, 86–88, 87n, 95; report, 111–114, 116, 118

Citizens Committee for Neighborhood Schools (CCNS): 93–95, 108–111, 133–135

Citizens for Excellence in Education (CEE), 13, 163, 169; organization of, 137–140; upper-middle class nature of, 137; and the tax proposal, 158; and the liberal board, 189–190

Coleman Report, 44

Conformity, pressures toward, 176–183, 191

Congress of Racial Equality (CORE), 86, 95

Contra Costa County Committee on School District Organization, 23

Contra Costa Legal Services Foundation (CCLSF), 127, 163, 167

Cooper, John, 144, 147

Dahl, Robert, 101

Damerell, Reginald, 72, 116n, 200

Democratic theory: classical, 100–107, 198, 206–208; democratic elitism, 101–107, 198; pluralism, 101–107, 139, 198, 203

Dentler, Robert, 65

Dover School, 42, 43, 128–132

Downer Junior High School, boundary location, 79

Drug-abuse program, 172

Education: attainment in, 52, 53; aspirations in, 58–60, 59n; for women, 59–64; philosophy of,